Contents

GW00597336

Chapter 3 ∨

Managing Security with Windows 2000 Group Policy   29

Chapter 4

Securing Servers Based on Role   51

Microsoft®
Prescriptive Guidance

Security Operations Guide
for Windows® 2000 Server

ISBN: 0-7356-1823-2

Chapter 5

Patch Management   79

1

Introduction

Welcome to the Security Operations Guide for Windows 2000 Server. As the world becomes more and more connected, the vision of information being available anywhere, at any time, and on any device comes closer to reality. Businesses and their customers will only trust such an environment to store their sensitive data if they can be sure the environment is secure.

The 2001 Computer Crime and Security Survey by the Computer Security Institute (CSI) and the Federal Bureau of Investigation (FBI) showed 85 percent of large corporations and government agencies detected security breaches. The average loss over the year for each respondent was estimated to be over 2 million US dollars. Recent months have seen a spate of attacks against computer environments, many of them through the Internet, and many of them targeted at systems running the Microsoft® Windows® operating system. However, these are just the most public of the security issues facing organizations today. This guide will look at the many different threats to security in your environment and how you most effectively guard against them.

Whatever your environment, you are strongly advised to take security seriously. Many organizations make the mistake of underestimating the value of their information technology (IT) environment, generally because they exclude substantial indirect costs. If the attack is severe enough, this could be up to the value of your entire organization. For example, an attack in which your corporate website is subtly altered to announce fictional bad news could lead to the collapse of your corporation's stock price. When evaluating security costs, you should include the indirect costs associated with any attack, as well as the costs of lost IT functionality.

The most secure computer systems in the world are ones that are completely isolated from users or other systems. However, in the real world, we generally require functional computer systems that are networked, often using public networks. This guide will help you identify the risks inherent in a networked environment, help you to work out the level of security appropriate for your environment, and show you the steps necessary to achieve that level of security. Although targeted at the enterprise customer, much of this guide is appropriate for organizations of any size.

Microsoft Operations Framework (MOF)

For operations in your environment to be as efficient as possible, you must manage them effectively. To assist you, Microsoft has developed the Microsoft Operations Framework (MOF). This is essentially a collection of best practices, principles, and models providing you with operations guidance. Following MOF guidelines should help your mission critical production systems remain secure, reliable, available, supportable, and manageable using Microsoft products.

The MOF process model is split into four integrated quadrants, as follows:

- Changing
- Operating
- Supporting
- Optimizing

Together, the phases form a spiral life cycle (see Figure 1.1) that can apply to anything from a specific application to an entire operations environment with multiple data centers. In this case, you will be using MOF in the context of security operations.

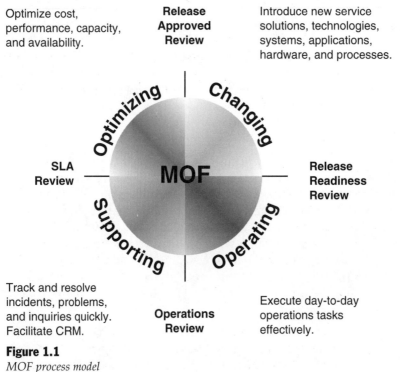

Optimize cost, performance, capacity, and availability.

Release Approved Review

Introduce new service solutions, technologies, systems, applications, hardware, and processes.

SLA Review

Release Readiness Review

Track and resolve incidents, problems, and inquiries quickly. Facilitate CRM.

Operations Review

Execute day-to-day operations tasks effectively.

Figure 1.1
MOF process model

The process model is supported by 20 service management functions (SMFs) and an integrated team model and risk model. Each quadrant is supported with a corresponding operations management review (also known as a review milestone), during which the effectiveness of that quadrant's SMFs are assessed.

It is not essential to be a MOF expert to understand and use this guide, but a good understanding of MOF principles will help you manage and maintain a reliable, available, and stable operations environment.

If you wish to learn more about MOF and how it can assist you in your enterprise, visit the Microsoft Operations Framework website. See the "More Information" section at the end of this chapter for details.

Get Secure and Stay Secure

In October 2001, Microsoft launched an initiative known as the Strategic Technology Protection Program (STPP). The aim of this program is to integrate Microsoft products, services, and support that focus on security. Microsoft sees the process of maintaining a secure environment as two related phases: Get Secure and Stay Secure.

Get Secure

The first phase is called Get Secure. To help your organization achieve an appropriate level of security, follow the Get Secure recommendations in the Microsoft Security Tool Kit, which can be accessed online (see the "More Information" section for details).

Stay Secure

The second phase is known as Stay Secure. It is one thing to create an environment that is initially secure. However, once your environment is up and running, it's entirely another to keep the environment secure over time, take preventative action against threats, and respond to them effectively when they do occur.

Scope of this Guide

This guide is focused explicitly on the operations required to create and maintain a secure environment on servers running Windows 2000. Windows 2000 Server has the following minimum system requirements:

Computer/Processor: 133 MHz or higher Pentium-compatible CPU

Memory: 256 megabytes (MB) of RAM recommended minimum [128 MB minimum supported; 4 gigabytes (GB) maximum]

Hard Disk: 2 GB hard disk with a minimum of 1.0 GB free space (Additional free hard disk space is required if you are installing over a network.)

CPU Support: Windows 2000 Server supports up to four CPUs on one machine

We examine specific roles defined for servers, but do not show in detail how to run specific applications in a secure manner.

When implementing security, there are many areas that you must design and implement. The diagram provides a high level view of these areas, the shaded areas are covered in this guide.

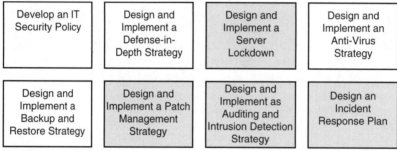

Figure 1.2
Security areas

The diagram shows the steps required to help make a server secure (Get Secure) and help keep it that way (Stay Secure). It also shows how the chapters of this guide will help you achieve those aims.

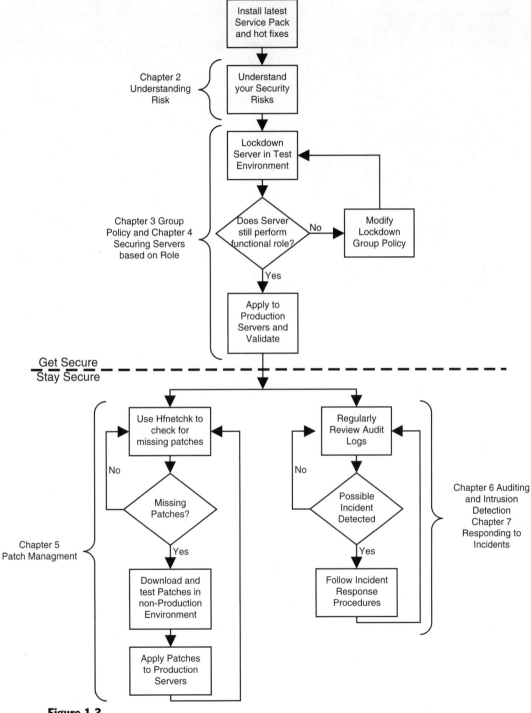

Figure 1.3
Security process flowchart

Note: This diagram is not meant to show every task that should be involved in your stay secure operational processes, such as running anti-virus software and performing regular back ups. Instead, it is intended to show the tasks discussed in detail in this guide.

You should use this guide as part of your overall security strategy, not as a complete reference to cover all aspects of creating and maintaining a secure environment.

Chapter Outlines

This guide consists of the following chapters, each of which takes you through a part of the security operations process. Each chapter is designed to be read, in whole or in part, according to your needs.

Chapter 2: Understanding Security Risk

Before you can attempt to make your environment secure, you have to understand threats, vulnerabilities, exploits, and countermeasures in the context of IT security. This chapter looks at these issues and examines business and technical decisions that will help you to manage security risk in your environment more effectively.

Chapter 3: Managing Security with Windows 2000 Group Policy

Many security settings are defined in Windows 2000 through Group Policy, aimed at controlling the behavior of objects on the local computer and in the Active Directory™ directory service. It is important to ensure that these policies are set appropriately, and that you monitor to ensure they are not changed without prior authorization. This chapter will look in detail at managing security using Group Policy.

Chapter 4: Securing Servers Based on Role

An application server, a file server and a web server all require different settings to maximize their security. This chapter looks at domain controllers and a number of different member server roles and shows the steps you should take to ensure that each of these roles are as secure as possible.

Note: This guide assumes that servers perform specific defined roles. If your servers do not match these roles, or you have multipurpose servers, you should use the settings defined here as a guideline for creating your own security templates to give you the functionality you require. However, you should bear in mind that the more functions each of your individual servers performs, the more vulnerable you are to attack.

Chapter 5: Patch Management

One of the main ways to guard against attack is to ensure your environment is kept up to date with all the necessary security patches. Patches may be required at the server and client level. This chapter shows you how you ensure you find out about new patches in a timely manner, implement them quickly and reliably throughout your organization, and monitor to ensure they are deployed everywhere.

Chapter 6: Auditing and Intrusion Detection

Not all attacks are obvious. Sometimes the more subtle attacks are more dangerous, because they go unnoticed and it is difficult to tell what changes have been made. This chapter shows how to audit your environment to give you the best chances of spotting attack, and looks at intrusion detection systems — software specifically designed to spot behavior that indicates an attack is occurring.

Chapter 7: Responding to Incidents

No matter how secure your environment, the risk of being attacked remains. Any sensible security strategy must include details on how your organization would respond to different types of attack. This chapter will cover the best ways to respond to different types of attack, and includes the steps you should take to report the incidents effectively. It also includes a case study showing a typical response to an incident.

Summary

This chapter has introduced you to this guide and summarized the other chapters in it. It has also introduced the Strategic Technology Protection Program (STTP). Now that you understand the organization of the guide, you can decide whether to read it from beginning to end, or whether you want to read selected portions. Remember that effective, successful security operations require effort in all areas, not just improvements in one, so you are best advised to read all chapters.

More Information

Symantec has created a parallel guide showing how to use their tools to implement the best practices described in this guide:

*http://securityresponse.symantec.com/avcenter/security/Content/security.articles
/security.fundamentals.html*

For more detail on how MOF can assist in your enterprise:

http://www.microsoft.com/business/services/mcsmof.asp

Microsoft Security Tool Kit: *http://www.microsoft.com/technet/treeview/default.asp?url=
/technet/security/tools/stkintro.asp*

Microsoft Strategic Technology Protection Program Website:

http://microsoft.com/security/mstpp.asp

Information on the Microsoft Security Notification Service:

http://www.microsoft.com/technet/treeview/default.asp?url=/technet/security/bulletin/notify.asp

2

Understanding Security Risk

As IT systems evolve, so do the security threats they face. If you are going to protect your environment effectively against attack, you need a thorough understanding of the dangers you are likely to encounter.

When identifying security threats, you should consider two main factors: 1) The types of attacks you are likely to face, and 2) Where those attacks may occur. Many organizations neglect the second factor, assuming a serious attack will only occur from outside (typically through their Internet connection). In the CSI/FBI Computer Crime and Security Survey, 31 percent of respondents cited their internal systems as a frequent point of attack. However, many companies may be unaware that internal attacks are occurring, mainly because they are not monitoring for them.

In this chapter, we examine the types of attack you may face. We will also look at some of the steps, both business and technical, you can take to minimize the threats to your environment.

Risk Management

There is no such thing as a completely secure and still useful IT environment. As you examine your environment, you will need to assess the risks you currently face, determine an acceptable level of risk, and maintain risk at or below that level. Risks are reduced by increasing the security of your environment.

As a general rule, the higher the level of security in an organization, the more costly it is to implement and the more likely that there will be reductions in functionality. After assessing the potential risks, you may have to reduce your level of security in favor of increased functionality and lowered cost.

For example, consider a credit card company that is considering implementing a fraud prevention system. If fraud costs the company 3 million dollars a year, but the fraud prevention system costs 5 million dollars a year to implement and maintain there is no direct financial benefit in installing the system. However, the company may suffer indirect losses worth far more than 3 million, such as loss of reputation and loss of consumer confidence. Therefore, the calculation is actually far more complex.

Sometimes, extra levels of security will result in more complex systems for users. An online bank may decide to use multiple levels of authentication for its users each time they access their account. However, if the authentication process is made too complex some customers will not bother to use the system, which could potentially cost more than the attacks the bank may suffer.

In order to understand the principles of risk management you need to understand some key terms used in the risk management process. These include resources, threats, vulnerabilities, exploits and countermeasures.

Resources

A resource is anything in your environment that you are trying to protect. This could include data, applications, servers, routers and even people. The purpose of security is to prevent your resources from being attacked.

An important part of risk management is to determine the value of your resources. You would not use standard door locks and a home alarm system to guard the Crown Jewels. Similarly, the value of your resources will generally determine the level of security appropriate to protect them.

Threats

A threat is a person, place, or thing that has the potential to access resources and cause harm. The table shows different types of threats and examples of them.

Table 2.1: Threats to Computing Environments

Type of Threat	Examples
Natural and Physical	Fire, Water, Wind, Earthquake Power Failure
Unintentional	Uninformed Employees Uninformed Customers
Intentional	Attackers Terrorists Industrial Spies Governments Malicious Code

Vulnerabilities

A vulnerability is a point where a resource is susceptible to attack. It can be thought of as a weakness. Vulnerabilities are often categorized as shown in the following table.

Table 2.2: Vulnerabilities in Computing Environments

Type of Vulnerability	Examples
Physical	Unlocked Doors
Natural	Broken Fire Suppression System
Hardware and Software	Out of date antivirus software
Media	Electrical Interference
Communication	Unencrypted Protocols
Human	Insecure helpdesk procedures

Note: The examples listed for threats and vulnerabilities may not apply to your organization as every organization differs.

Exploit

A resource may be accessed by a threat that makes use of a vulnerability in your environment. This type of attack is known as an exploit. The exploitation of resources can be performed in many ways. Some of the more common are given in the following table.

Table 2.3: Exploits in Computing Environments

Type of Exploit	Example
Technical Vulnerability Exploitation	Brute Force Attacks Buffer Overflows Misconfigurations Replay Attacks Session Hijacking
Information Gathering	Address Identification OS Identification Port Scanning Service and Application Probing Vulnerability Scanning Response Analysis User Enumeration Document Grinding Wireless Leak Social Engineering
Denial of Service	Physical Damage Removal of Resources Resource Modification Resource Saturation

When a threat uses a vulnerability to attack a resource, some severe consequences can result. The table shows some of the results of exploits you may encounter in your environment and examples of them.

Table 2.4: Results of Exploits

Results of Exploit	Examples
Loss of Confidentiality	Unauthorized access Privilege escalation Impersonation or identity theft
Loss of Integrity	Data Corruption Disinformation
Loss of Availability	Denial of Service

Relationship Between Threats, Vulnerabilities, and Risk

Each threat and vulnerability identified within your organization should be qualified and ranked using a standard, such as low, medium, or high. The ranking will vary between organizations and sometimes even within an organization. For example, the threat of earthquakes is significantly higher for offices near a major fault line than for elsewhere. Similarly, the vulnerability of physical damage to equipment would be very high for an organization producing highly sensitive and fragile electronics while a construction company may have a lower vulnerability level.

Note: Job Aid 1: Threat Analysis Table can be used to help you evaluate threats and how much impact they may have on your organization.

The level of risk in your organization increases with the level of threat and vulnerability. This is shown in the following diagram.

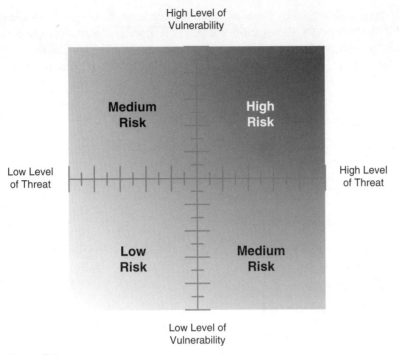

Figure 2.1
Risk matrix

Countermeasures

Countermeasures are deployed to counteract threats and vulnerabilities, therefore reducing the risk in your environment. For example, an organization producing fragile electronics may deploy physical security countermeasures such as securing equipment to the building's foundation or adding buffering mechanisms. These countermeasures reduce the likelihood that an earthquake could cause physical damage to their assets. Residual risk is what remains after all countermeasures have been applied to reduce threats and vulnerabilities.

Defense in Depth

To reduce risk in your environment, you should use a defense-in-depth strategy to protect resources from external and internal threats. Defense in depth (sometimes referred to as security in depth or multilayered security) is taken from a military term used to describe the layering of security countermeasures to form a cohesive security environment without a single point of failure. The security layers that form your defense-in-depth strategy should include deploying protective measures from your external routers all the way through to the location of your resources, and all points in between.

By deploying multiple layers of security, you help ensure that if one layer is compromised, the other layers will provide the security needed to protect your resources. For example, the compromise of an organization's firewall should not provide an attacker unfettered access to the organization's most sensitive data. Ideally each layer should provide different forms of countermeasures to prevent the same exploit method from being used at multiple layers.

The diagram shows an effective defense-in-depth strategy:

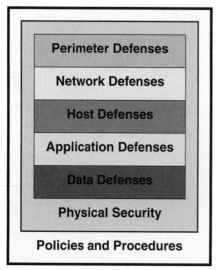

Figure 2.2
Defense-in-depth strategy

It is important to remember that your resources are not just data, but anything in your environment which is susceptible to attack. As part of your risk management strategy, you should examine the resources you are protecting, and determine if you have sufficient protection for all of them. Of course, the amount of security you can deploy will depend upon your risk assessment and the cost and benefits analysis of deploying countermeasures. However, the aim is to ensure that an attacker will need significant knowledge, time, and resources to bypass all countermeasures and gain access to your resources.

Note: Exactly how you deploy defense in depth will depend upon the specifics of your environment. Make sure that you reassess your defense-in-depth strategy as your environment changes.

It is worth examining each layer of a defense-in-depth strategy in more detail.

Data Defenses

For many companies, one of their most valuable resources is data. If that data fell into the hands of competitors, or became corrupted, they could be in serious trouble.

At the client level, data stored locally is particularly vulnerable. If a laptop is stolen, the data can be backed up, restored elsewhere and read, even if the criminal is unable to log on to the system.

Data can be protected in a number of ways including data encryption using the Encrypting File Service (EFS) or third party encryption and modifying discretionary access control lists on the files.

Application Defenses

As another layer of defense, application hardening is an essential part of any security model. Many applications use the security subsystem of Windows 2000 to provide security. However, it is the developer's responsibility to incorporate security within the application to provide additional protection to the areas of the architecture that the application can access. An application exists within the context of the system, so you should always consider the security of your entire environment when looking at application security.

Each application in your organization should be thoroughly tested for security compliance in a test environment before you allow it to be run in a production setting.

Host Defenses

You should evaluate every host in your environment and create policies that limit each server to only those tasks it has to perform. Doing so creates another security barrier that an attacker would need to circumvent before they could do any damage. Chapter 4, "Securing Servers Based on Role," provides policies which increase the security for five common Windows 2000 server roles.

One way of doing this is to create individual policies based on the classification and type of data contained on each server. For example, an organization's policy might stipulate that all Web servers are for public use and, therefore, can contain only public information. Their database servers are designated as company confidential, which means that the information must be protected at all costs, resulting in the classifications outlined in the table on the next page.

Table 2.5: Classification of Servers

Value	Definition
Public Use	Distribution of this material is not limited. This includes marketing information, sales materials, and information cleared for release to the public. Data on public Internet servers should be for public use.
Internal Use Only	Disclosure of this information is safe for internal distribution, but could cause measurable damage to the organization if released publicly. At least one firewall should be placed between this information and the Internet.
Company Confidential	Disclosure of this information would cause serious damage to the organization as a whole. This information is of the most sensitive nature and is exposed only on a need-to-know basis. At least two firewalls should be placed between this information and the Internet.

Network Defenses

You may have a series of networks in your organization and should evaluate each individually to ensure that they are appropriately secured. If a router is successfully attacked, it may deny service to entire network segments.

You should look at the legitimate traffic on your networks, and block any traffic which is not required. You may also want to consider using IPSec to encrypt the packets on your internal networks, and SSL for external communication. You should also monitor for packet sniffers on the network, which should only be used under strict controls. *How?*

Perimeter Defenses

Protecting the perimeter of your network is the most important aspect of stopping attack from outside. If your perimeter remains secure, your internal network is protected from external attacks. Your organization should have some type of secure device protecting each access point into the network. Each device should be evaluated, the types of traffic to allow decided, and then a security model developed to block all other traffic.

Firewalls are an important part of perimeter defense. You will need one or more firewalls in place, to ensure that you minimize attacks from the outside, along with auditing and intrusion detection to make sure that you become aware of attacks if they do occur. For more information on auditing and intrusion detection see Chapter 6, "Auditing and Intrusion Detection."

How? You should also remember that for networks allowing remote access, the perimeter may include staff laptops or even home PCs. You will need to ensure that these computers meet your security requirements before they can connect to the network.

Physical Security

Any environment where unauthorized users can gain physical access to computers is inherently insecure. A very effective denial of service attack is simply removing the power supply from a server or taking the disk drives. Data theft (and denial of service) can occur by someone stealing a server or even a laptop.

You should consider physical security as fundamental to your overall security strategy. A first priority will be to physically secure your server locations. This could be server rooms within your building, or entire data centers.

You should also be looking at access to the buildings in your organization. If someone can gain access to a building, they may have many opportunities to launch an attack without even being able to log on to the network. These could include:

- Denial of service (for example, plugging a laptop into the network which is a DHCP server, or disconnecting the power to a server)
- Data theft (for example, stealing a laptop, or packet sniffing the internal network)
- Running malicious code (for example, launching a worm from within the organization)

- Theft of critical security information (for example, backup tapes, operations manuals and network diagrams)

As part of your risk management strategy you should determine the level of physical security appropriate to your environment. Possible physical security measures include some or all of the following.

- Physically securing all areas of the building (could include keycards, biometric devices and security guards)
- Requiring guests to be escorted at all times
- Requiring that guests check in all computing devices when they arrive
- Requiring all employees register any portable devices they own
- Physically securing all desktops and laptops to tables
- Requiring that all data storage devices are registered before they are removed from the building
- Placing servers in separate rooms that only administrators can enter
- Redundant Internet connections, power, fire suppression, and so on.
- Protecting against natural disasters and terrorist attack
- Securing access to areas that could allow a denial of service attack to occur (for example, areas where wiring runs out of the main building)

Policies and Procedures

Almost all the measures described so far are aimed at preventing unauthorized access to systems. However, there will, of course, be people in your environment who need high level access to systems. Any security strategy will be seriously flawed unless you can ensure that these people will not misuse the rights they have been granted.

Before employing new staff in your organization, you should ensure that they undergo a security screening process, with more rigorous screening for those employees who will be granted greater access to your systems.

For existing staff, it is critical that they are made aware of your security policies and what they are allowed to do or not do (and preferably why). This is important for two reasons. Firstly, if your staff is unaware of what is forbidden, they may well perform actions that unwittingly compromise the security of your environment. Secondly, if a member of your staff maliciously attacks your IT environment and this is not explicitly forbidden in company policy, it can be very difficult to take action against that person.

In a Windows 2000-based environment you can control very precisely the administrative rights your users have. You should ensure that you tightly define the scope of administrative rights that should be available to each member of your IT staff. No member of your staff should have more administrative access than is strictly required for their job.

Notifying your users about security may consist of an orientation program followed by regular reminders and prominently displayed updates to security procedures. It is vital that staff members realize that every member of the organization plays a role in keeping it secure.

Note: Job Aid 2: Top Security Blunders shows a list of common security blunders that can occur in any organization. These will severely increase the risk to your organization. As you define your security policies, you should ensure that you minimize the likelihood of these security blunders occurring.

Common Attack Methods and Prevention Measures

As part of your defense-in-depth strategy you need to understand the methods employed by attackers and defend against the most common attacks. This section looks at a number of types of attack and suggests steps for protecting your environment against them.

Note: Job Aid 3: Attacks and Countermeasures includes a table of common technical vulnerability exploitations and countermeasures that you can deploy for each.

Information Gathering

Attackers are always looking to find information about your environment. Information is sometimes useful in its own right; at other times it is a means to getting at further information and resources.

The key to preventing information gathering is to restrict unauthorized access to your resources from outside. Methods to ensure this include:

- Ensuring that only specific, identified devices on the network allow remote access connectivity. A modem-sweep utility should check all company prefixes, looking for unauthorized devices. Remote access devices can also be detected by activating scanning detection in the telephony system when available.

- Turning off NetBIOS over TCP/IP, including ports 135, 137, 139, and 445, on computers that directly connect to the Internet through the outside firewall. This makes it more difficult for outsiders to use standard networking to connect to servers.

- Enabling only ports 80 and 443 on both of the Internet-facing network adapters and the firewall for traffic destined for a Web farm. This eliminates most port-based reconnaissance techniques.

- Reviewing the information on the public Web site to ensure that:

  - E-mail addresses used on the site are not administrative accounts.

  - The network's technology is not specified.

  - General company information posted there is appropriate and cannot be used to discover or infer characteristics of the security system. This type of information includes current events and recent happenings. For example, if the Web site announces that your company has just acquired another firm, attackers may target the new acquisition in hopes that its network was hastily connected to the new corporate network and is therefore less secure.

- Reviewing employee postings to Usenet groups to evaluate the type of information that they expose.

- Managing the type of content placed in the Web site's source code to prevent an attacker from reviewing this code (a technique sometimes referred to as source sifting) to obtain valuable information. Some of the things the security team should look for in the source code include improper comments, embedded passwords, and hidden tags.

- Reviewing the information provided for the general public for your IP address and domain name registrations.

- Ensuring that an attacker cannot interrogate the DNS for the reference network or coax it into performing a complete zone transfer. By dumping all the records in the DNS, an attacker can get a good look at the computers that are most easily targeted. To prevent DNS interrogation, you can assign rights to the Windows 2000 DNS server by using the **Notify** option and enabling zone transfers only to authorized servers. Another approach is to implement a read-only DNS and put policies and procedures in place to update it.

- Reviewing the Site Security Handbook (RFC 2196) for information about important policy considerations. A company that does business with the public must expose some level of information. It is important to provide only what is required, not information that can be used maliciously.

- Managing the type of information supplied to individuals when they attempt to probe the network using utilities such as traceroute These utilities, which use the time-to-live (TTL) parameter, are used to follow the route of an IP packet from one host to the next; they then use the results to build a picture of the network.

Note: RFC 2196 is available from the Request for Comments Web site listed in the "More Information" section at the end of this chapter.

Limiting the Ability to Scan and Get Valuable Information

Both Transmission Control Protocol (TCP) and User Datagram Protocol (UDP) use ports to communicate. By using port scanners, attackers can discover the servers in your environment that are listening, and then use this information to discover vulnerabilities.

There are a number of scans that are useful to attackers. These can be used to gain information on listening ports, protocols present, or even the host's operating system (OS) and version status. Identifying the ports, protocols, and OS of a host will help discover many vulnerabilities that might not be discovered without scanning the device.

The table shows some of the more important scanning methods, what they do, and where they may be valuable:

Table 2.6: Scanning Methods and Their Uses

Scanning Method	How it works	Why it is useful
Internet Control Message Protocol (ICMP) Echo or Ping	Sends ICMP port 0 packets to the receiving system. If the system allows responses to ICMP echoes it will send an ICMP reply to the scanning system showing that the system is alive and listening to network traffic.	A ping scan is used to identify hosts listening on the network. It does not identify listening ports or protocols other than ICMP. Many security filtering devices will block ICMP echo requests, therefore preventing pings through the perimeter.

Scanning Method	How it works	Why it is useful
TCP Connect or Three-Way Handshake	Uses the standard three-way handshake to verify a connection to a listening TCP port.	Very good if you will not be going through TCP filtering security devices such as a firewall or a packet filtering router.
TCP Spoofed Connection Request (SYN)	Uses the first two steps of the three-way handshake. The scanning system sends a packet with the reset (RST) flag for the last step instead of a status acknowledge (ACK) thereby not establishing a complete connection.	Less likely to be detected or filtered by security devices since a connection is never established. Somewhat slower than a TCP connect scan.
TCP Finish (FIN)	All flags are turned off except for the FIN flag. Packets of this type received on listening ports usually do not send a response whereas a non-listening port will usually send a RST packet. Ports not responding are those that are listening.	May bypass systems or security devices listening for SYN only packets as seen with a TCP SYN scan. May not get accurate results from Windows-based systems making it more difficult to ascertain open ports on those systems.
Fragmented packet	TCP packets are broken into fragments to be re-assembled at the destination while using one of the previous scanning techniques.	Some security devices including intrusion detection systems may have a difficult time with rebuilding these packet streams. Can sometimes bypass filtering devices or even cause them to crash. Can cause a significant load on these devices.
Ident retrieval	An Ident request is sent after a TCP connection (three-way handshake) has been established to determine which account is associated with the listening port process.	This type of scan will not identify listening ports, but it can identify accounts and their associated services. Microsoft operating systems will not provide this information.

(continued)

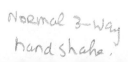

Scanning Method	How it works	Why it is useful
File Transfer Protocol (FTP) Proxy Scan	The original RFC for FTP designed a proxy type service that allows a user to make a connection to an FTP server and request the FTP server to initiate a file transfer to any other system. An FTP proxy scan uses this design flaw to proxy port connection requests to other systems.	May be useful in scanning systems hidden behind firewalls. The discovery of a system that allows this is a vulnerability in itself, in that it passes traffic to locations not allowed by your security policies or security devices.
UDP	UDP is a connectionless protocol, meaning that the sending system does not expect a response from the destination box. A system performing a UDP scan will receive responses only from non-listening ports.	UDP ports are often not filtered by security devices or have limited filtering, due to their connectionless nature. Often, UDP services such as DNS and simple network management protocol (SNMP) are not securely implemented and are often allowed to pass through security perimeters. Slow connections or those with high packet loss may inaccurately show most ports open.
OS Detection	OS detection can be performed in a number of ways but often the most accurate is to compare TCP responses from the device to a list of known system types. Some components that are used to determine host information include the TTL, TCP sequence numbers, fragmentation, FIN and ACK response, undefined flags response, windows size, ICMP responses, and multiple TCP options.	Often OS detection scan will bypass many filtering devices with the exception of proxying firewalls since the firewall is what is actually sending the responses. More than one OS type may be returned and results may not be accurate. Firewalls or routers often deny ICMP based OS detection scans.

While scanning is used by attackers, you should also be aware of any vulnerabilities they detect. It is therefore a good idea to implement strictly controlled scanning in your environment.

To protect your network from scanning, you should at a minimum do the following:

- Identify required ports; all members of the security committee should concur before opening any other ports.
- Implement a network intrusion detection system.   (IDS)
- Stop all services on the system that are not required. Details on the services that are stopped in the five Windows 2000 server roles are covered in Chapter 4 "Securing Servers Based on Role."
- Apply all current system patches. Details on how to keep current on system patches can be found in Chapter 5, "Patch Management."

Technical Vulnerability Exploitation

Attackers will attempt to exploit technical vulnerabilities in your environment in order to gain access to your systems and elevate their privileges. There are a number of methods that may be used. In this section we list some of the key methods and show how to guard against them.

Session Hijacking

Session hijacking tools allow an attacker to interrupt, end, or steal a session in progress. These types of attacks tend to focus on session-based applications. Many session hijacking tools can view multiple sessions simultaneously. The best solution to protect the architecture against session hijacking is to use encryption.

Preventing DNS Poisoning

DNS servers are a vital part of any Windows 2000-based network. All network clients query the DNS servers to locate servers with which they need to communicate. When attacking DNS, an attacker can use DNS poisoning. For example, an attacker can use a variety of penetration techniques to overwrite the cache file of the DNS server with malicious information. As a result, when a user queries the production DNS, the user is forwarded to a bogus DNS server that the attacker controls and can use to damage the system. The following approaches can be used to prevent attacks on the DNS:

- Use different DNS servers to resolve requests for the internal network and ensure that these DNS servers do not respond to queries from outside computers. This is referred to as split-split DNS.
- Use a read-only DNS that disallows any updates.
- Secure the DNS database by using Active Directory security and only allowing secure DNS updates.
- Enable DNS cache poison protection in the advanced setting of the Windows 2000 DNS configuration.

URL String Attacks

Attackers are now starting to focus their efforts on attacks that traverse port 80. One form of this is type of attack is to create a URL string that uses a Unicode Translation Format-8 (UTF-8) encoded version of the back or forward slash (\ or /); an example of such a string is, %c0%af. This type of attack allows an attacker to traverse the remote systems directory structure, gain valuable server or network information, or even run a program remotely.

For example, the Nimda worm uses a UTF-encoded URL string to launch a Trivial File Transfer Protocol (TFTP) session on the remote server and download its payload to the compromised computer. The worm then installs its own TFTP server, downloads the rest of its payload, and begins replicating itself in a variety of ways, such as launching mass mailings, embedding an .eml file within a Web site, and attacking open network shares.

The first step in applying a defense-in-depth strategy against a URL string attack is to learn as much about the attack as possible and to make sure that you are up to date on current patch levels. More information on staying current on patches can be found in Chapter 5, "Patch Management."

More information on the Nimda worm and specifically guarding against it can be found on TechNet (See the "More Information" section at the end of this chapter for further details).

Attacking the Security Accounts Manager File

By attacking the Security Accounts Manager (SAM) file, an attacker can potentially gain access to usernames and passwords. Once an attacker has access to this information, he can use it to gain apparently legitimate access to resources on your network. Managing the SAM file is therefore an important step in preventing attacks. Methods to achieve this include:

- Using System Key (Syskey) to enable additional encryption on the SAM file.
- Disabling local area network (LAN) Manager Authentication and storage of the LAN Manager hash through a policy, and using other forms of authentication (such as certificates and biometrics).
- Establishing and enforcing a complex password policy.

Buffer Overflows

Buffer overflows are a very dangerous technique employed by attackers to gain access to a system. Attackers attempt to put too much information into a container to see if they can get the overflow to act in a meaningful way. For example, if the program being attacked does not perform proper bounds checking, it overflows and allows the attacker to execute functions of their choosing. Often these overflows run in the context of local system accounts that have full administrative rights.

Many overflow attacks are well documented and can be downloaded easily from the Web. The most common types of these attacks are stack-based buffer overflow attacks. The overflow overwrites the whole stack, including pointers. The attacker takes advantage of this by tuning the amount of data placed in the overflow. The attacker then sends computer-specific code to execute a command and a new address for the return pointer. Lastly, the attacker uses the address, which points back to the stack, to execute their program instructions when the system returns to the stack.

To control buffer overflow attacks, you will need to:

- Keep systems up to date with the latest service packs, hot fixes, and patches. See Chapter 5, "Patch Management" for best practices.
- Implement good coding practices and follow standard guidelines for bounds checking. There are many resources on this topic; for example, *Writing Secure Code* by Michael Howard and David LeBlanc (Microsoft Press; ISBN: 0-7356-1588-8).

Denial of Service Attacks

An attacker does not necessarily have to gain access to a system in order to cause significant problems. Denial of Service (DoS) attacks involve tying up the resources of a system sufficiently to prevent it from performing its normal function. Examples would include using up all the network connections on a server, or ensuring that a mail server has to deal with vastly more mail than it is designed to handle. DoS attacks may be due to a direct attack, or may be caused by viruses, worms or Trojan horses.

Distributed Denial of Service (DDoS) attacks involve installing programs known as zombies on various computers in advance of the attack. A command is issued to these zombies, which launch the attack on behalf of the attacker, thus hiding their tracks. The zombies themselves are often installed using worms.

The real danger from a DDoS attack is that the attacker uses many victim computers as host computers to control other zombies that initiate the attack. When the system that is overwhelmed tries to trace back the attack, it receives a set of spoofed addresses generated by a series of zombies.

The following defensive steps will help you prevent these types of attacks:

- Keep systems updated with the latest security patches. See Chapter 5, "Patch Management" for best practices.
- Block large ping packets at the router and firewall, stopping them from reaching the perimeter network.
- Apply anti-spoof filters on the router; that is, block any incoming packet that has a source address equal to an address on the internal network.

- Filter the ICMP messages on the firewall and router (although this could affect some management tools).
- Develop a defense plan with your Internet service provider (ISP) that enables a rapid response to an attack that targets the bandwidth between your ISP and your perimeter network.
- Disable the response to directed broadcasts.   *How?*
- Apply proper router and firewall filtering.
- Use an IDS system to check for unusual traffic and generate an alert if it detects any. Configure IDS to generate an alert if it detects ICMP_ECHOREPLY without associated ICMP_ECHO packets.

DoS and DDoS are the most common types of attacks on the Internet. Each week, more DoS attacks are documented and added to bug tracking databases. You should ensure that you always remain current on these attacks and how you can guard against them.

Backdoor Attacks

To prevent attackers from downloading system information, you must protect against an attacker using a Trojan horse to install a backdoor on the system. This is usually more of an issue on the client than on a completely secured server. However, an attacker can use such a mechanism to attack a user or an administrator's workstation and then use that system to launch attacks on a production perimeter network.

For example, Back Orifice 2000 is a backdoor program that allows attackers to remotely control a computer over the network, capture keystrokes, and use the information to become a user of a workstation on the network. Many virus checkers detect Back Orifice; however, new versions of Back Orifice create different mutations that are not detected by virus checkers. It also runs in stealth mode and does not show up in the task list because the size of its footprint is less than 100 kilobytes (KB). Back Orifice is only one of many backdoor programs. You can help prevent these types of attacks from succeeding by:

- Running a complete virus scan and keeping the virus tool up to date with the latest signatures.
- Being careful with all content sent over e-mail, and restricting the execution of unknown attachments.
- Running tools, such as the Internet Security Systems (ISS) scanner, to scan the entire network for the presence of attacker tools, such as Back Orifice; making sure that the scanner database is kept up to date.
- Accepting only signed Microsoft ActiveX® controls.
- Educating users about the dangers of installing unknown programs, launching questionable attachments, or downloading unsigned or unknown Internet content.

Malicious Code

Any executable code is potentially a risk to your organization. Malicious code can take the form of damaging code which spreads within and between organizations (for example through e-mail) or it can be code deliberately run from inside the organization for malicious purposes.

Malicious code can be narrowed down to four major types:

- Viruses
- Worms
- Trojan horses
- Other malicious code

Table 2.7: Types of Malicious Code

Malicious Code Type	Description
Virus	Infects another program, boot sector, partition sector or file that supports macros, by inserting itself or attaching itself to that medium. It then replicates to other computers from that point. Viruses may just replicate, but many will also do damage to the systems they infect.
Worm	Copies itself, from one disk drive to another, or across a network by using e-mail or some other transport mechanism. It does not need to modify its host in order to spread. It may do damage and compromise the security of the computer.
Trojan Horse	Does not replicate on its own, but its malicious functionality is hidden within other programs which appear to have some use, so will tend to be passed around (often it may be in the form of a joke program). Once present on a system it will typically do damage or compromise the security of the computer, which can be the first step to allowing unauthorized access.
Other Malicious Code	Executable code that either intentionally or unintentionally causes damage to your environment. An example is a batch file that loops, and on each loop uses up system resources until the computer can no longer function normally.

Anti-virus utilities will prevent much malicious code from running, but not all. If you prevent access to CD-ROMs, floppy disks and other i/o devices, you will further protect against much of this code, but you will not stop code that is written on internal systems. Code may also be e-mailed to someone inside your organization. Even if the attachment type is not allowed, this can easily be circumvented by changing the file extension to get it into the organization and changing it back to run it.

Protecting key system and data files from unauthorized access is a major part of guarding against any hostile attack code. You will also need to make sure that you protect Active Directory and its components.

Summary

This chapter has shown the most significant threats to your environment and some actions you can take to protect against them. As you read through the following chapters you will see more detailed information as to how to protect your system against attack, how to spot if you are being attacked, and what to do if an attack occurs.

More Information

For more information from Symantec on Defense in Depth, see:

http://securityresponse.symantec.com/avcenter/security/Content/security.articles /defense.in.depth.html

Writing Secure Code by Michael Howard and David LeBlanc (Microsoft Press; ISBN: 0-7356-1588-8).

Information on the Nimda worm and guarding against it:

http://www.microsoft.com/technet/treeview/default.asp?url=/technet/security/topics /nimda.asp

Requests for Comments (RFCs) are available from:

http://www.rfc-editor.org/

TcP

- Web (80, 443)
- mail (25)
- FTP (21)

UDP

- DNS (53)
- Netbios (135, 139)
- SNMP (161)

3

Managing Security with Windows 2000 Group Policy

After you have determined the level of risk appropriate for your environment and established your overall security policy, it is time to start securing your environment. In a Windows 2000-based environment, this is mainly achieved through Group Policy.

In this chapter we will show how to set up Group Policy objects (GPOs) with security templates to define security settings in your Windows 2000-based environment and we will discuss a simple organizational unit (OU) structure that will support the use of these GPOs.

Warning: Before implementing the security templates discussed in this chapter in a production environment, you must first test the security templates thoroughly in a lab to ensure your servers continue to function as expected.

Importance of Using Group Policy

The goal of security policies is to define the procedures for configuring and managing security in your environment. Windows 2000 Group Policy can help you to implement technical recommendations in your security policy for all the workstations and servers in your Active Directory domains. You can use Group Policy in conjunction with your OU structure to define specific security settings for certain server roles.

If you use Group Policy to implement security settings, you can ensure that any changes made to a policy will apply to all servers using that policy and that new servers will automatically obtain the new settings.

How Group Policy is Applied

To use Group Policy safely and efficiently, it is very important to understand how it is applied. A user or computer object can be subject to multiple GPOs. These are applied sequentially, and the settings accumulate, except in the case of a conflict, where, by default, settings in later policies override those in earlier ones.

The first policy to be applied is the local GPO. Every computer running Windows 2000 has a local GPO stored on it. By default, only nodes under Security Settings are configured. Settings in other parts of the local GPO's namespace are neither enabled nor disabled. The local GPO is stored on each server in %systemroot%\System32\GroupPolicy.

After the local GPO, subsequent GPOs are applied at the site, domain, parent OU and finally child OU. The diagram shows how each policy is applied:

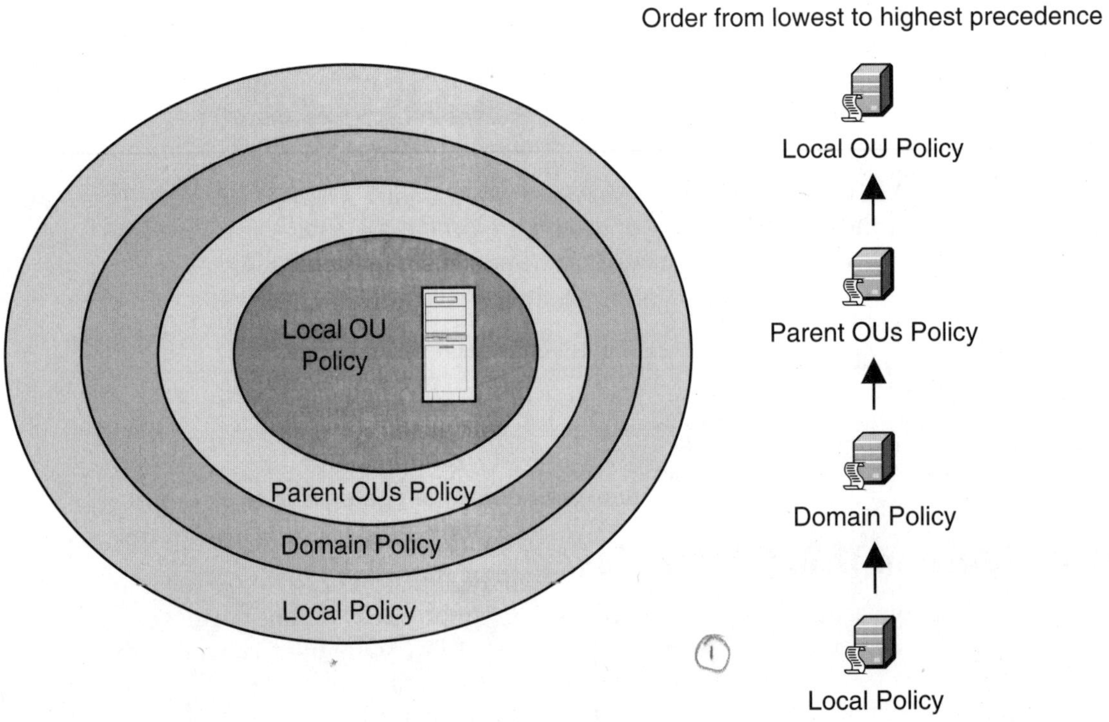

Figure 3.1
GPO application hierarchy

If there are multiple GPOs defined at each level, an administrator will set the order in which they are applied.

A user or computer will apply the settings defined in a Group Policy if a) the Group Policy is applied to their container and b) they appear in the Discretionary Access Control List (DACL) for the GPO with at least **Apply Group Policy** permission.

Note: By default, the built-in group, Authenticated Users, has the **Apply Group Policy** permission. This group contains all domain users and computers

Ensuring Group Policy is Applied

Group Policy settings are located (in part) in Active Directory. This means that changes to Group Policy are not applied immediately. Domain controllers first need to replicate Group Policy changes to other domain controllers. This will take up to 15 minutes within a site and significantly longer to replicate to other sites. Once changes have been replicated, there is a further time period (five minutes for domain controllers and 90 minutes plus or minus an offset of 30 minutes for other computers) before the changes in the policy are refreshed on the destination computer.

If you wish, you can force either of these actions to occur immediately.

▶ To force domain controller replication

1. Open **Active Directory Sites and Services**, expand **Sites**, expand the **<site name>**, and then expand **Servers**.

2. Expand both **<DC name 1>** and **<DC name 2>** and then, for each server select **NTDS Settings**.

3. In the right pane, right-click the connection object name and select **Replicate Now**. This will force replication immediately between both domain controllers.

4. Repeat steps 2 and 3 for each domain controller.

▶ To refresh policy manually on a server

At the server command prompt, type **Secedit /refreshpolicy machine_policy / enforce**. This command tells the server to check Active Directory for any updates to the policy and, if there are any, to download them immediately.

▶ To verify the effective policy settings

1. Start **Local Security Policy**.

2. Under **Security Settings**, click **Local Policies**, and then click **Security Options**.

3. In the right pane, view the **Effective Settings** column to verify that the correct security settings have been applied.

Note: As you will be applying security settings using Group Policy, it is very important you have a thorough understanding of their properties and interactions. The Microsoft white paper– Windows 2000 Group Policy, provides more detailed information on how they are deployed. For more details, see the "More Information" section at the end of this chapter.

Group Policy Structure

Group Policy configuration settings are stored in two locations:

- GPOs – located in Active Directory
- Security template files – located in the local file system

Changes made to the GPO are saved directly in Active Directory, whereas changes made to the security template files must then be imported back into the GPO within Active Directory before the changes can be applied.

Note: This operations guide provides you with templates which can be used to modify your GPOs. If you make changes and modify the GPOs directly, they will be out of sync with the template files. You would therefore be advised to modify the template files and import them back into the GPO.

Windows 2000 comes with a number of security templates. The following templates can be applied in a low security environment.

- Basicwk.inf–for Windows 2000 Professional
- Basicsv.inf–for Windows 2000 Server
- Basicdc.inf–for Windows 2000-based domain controllers

To implement higher security to Windows 2000-based computers, further templates are provided. These provide additional security settings to the basic templates:

- Securedc.inf and Hisecdc.inf – for domain controllers
- Securews.inf and Hisecws.inf – for member servers and workstations

These templates are considered incremental templates because the basic templates must be applied before the incremental templates can be added. For this guide we have created new security templates, using Hisecdc.inf and Hisecws.inf as the starting points. The aim is to create a very restrictive environment, which you can then selectively open up to provide the functionality you require, while still keeping security of premium importance.

Note: The Windows 2000 default security templates are stored as .inf files in the %SystemRoot%\Security\Templates folder.

Security Template Format

Template files are text-based files. Changes to the template files can be made from the MMC snap-in Security Templates or by using a text editor such as Notepad. The following table shows how the policy sections maps to sections of the template files.

Table 3.1: Security Template Sections Corresponding to Group Policy Settings

Policy Section	Template Section
Account Policy	[System Access]
Audit Policy	[System Log] [Security Log] [Application Log]
User Rights	[Privilege Rights]
Security Options	[Registry Values]
Event Log	[Event Audit]
Restricted Groups	[Group Membership]
System Services	[Service General Setting]
Registry	[Registry Keys]
File System	[File Security]

Some sections within the security template file, such as the [File Security] and [Registry Keys], contain specific access control lists (ACLs). These ACLs are text strings, defined by the Security Descriptor Definition Language (SDDL). More information on editing security templates and on SDDL can be found on MSDN. For further details, see the "More Information" section at the end of this chapter.

Test Environment

It is vital that you thoroughly assess any changes to the security of your IT systems in a test environment before you make any changes to your production environment. Your test environment should mimic your production environment as closely as possible. At the very least, it should include multiple domain controllers and each member server role you will have in the production environment.

Testing is necessary to establish that your environment is still functional after you make changes, but is also vital to ensure that you have increased the level of security as intended. You should thoroughly validate all changes and perform vulnerability assessments on the test environment.

Note: Before anyone performs vulnerability assessments in your organization, you should ensure that they have obtained written permission to do so.

Checking Your Domain Environment

Before implementing Group Policy in your production environment, it is important that the domain environment is stable and working properly. Some of the key areas in Active Directory that should be verified are DNS servers, domain controller replication, and time synchronization. You should also use a test environment to help ensure a stable production environment.

Verifying DNS Configuration

Name resolution by DNS is critical for servers and domain controllers to function properly. When multiple DNS servers are implemented for a domain, each DNS server should be tested. You should perform the following tests:

- On domain controllers:
  - Run dcdiag /v and netdiag /v using the verbose option to test DNS on each domain controller and review the output for any errors. DCDIAG and NETDIAG can be found on the Windows 2000 installation CD under the Support Tools directory.
  - Stop and start the Net Logon service and check the Event Log for any errors. The Net Logon service will dynamically register the service records in DNS for that domain controller and will produce error messages if it is not able to successfully register DNS records. These service records can be found in the file netlogon.dns located in the %SystemRoot%\System32\Config directory.
- On member servers, verify that DNS is operating correctly by using nslookup or running netdiag /v.

Domain Controller Replication

It is important that replication between multiple domain controllers is working properly before implementing Group Policy. If replication is not working correctly then changes made to Group Policy will not be applied to all domain controllers. This can create inconsistency between servers that are looking for Group Policy updates on domain controllers. Servers will be updated if they are pointing to the domain controller that the change was made on, while servers pointing to domain controllers that are still waiting for the Group Policy to be replicated will not be updated.

Forcing and Verifying Replication using Repadmin

Repadmin is a command-line tool included in the Support directory on the Windows 2000 CD. You can use repadmin to determine the directory replication partners of the destination server, and then issue a command to synchronize the source server with the destination server. This is done using the object globally unique identifier (GUID) of the source server.

▶ **To use repadmin to force replication between two domain controllers**

1. At a command prompt from a domain controller, type the following:

   repadmin /showreps <destination_server_name>

2. Under the Inbound Neighbors section of the output, find the directory partition that needs synchronization and locate the source server with which the destination is to be synchronized. Note the object GUID value of the source server.

3. Initiate replication by entering the following command:

   repadmin /sync

   <directory_partition_DN> <destination_server_name> <source_server_objectGuid>

Note: Once you have the object GUID of each domain controller, you could create a batch script that uses the repadmin tool to initiate replication between servers and provide status on whether the replication is successful.

Centralize Security Templates

It is very important that the security templates used for production are stored in a secure location that can only be accessed by the administrators responsible for implementing Group Policy. By default, security templates are stored in the %SystemRoot%\security\templates folder on each domain controller. This folder is not replicated across multiple domain controllers. Therefore you will need to select a domain controller to hold the master copy of the security templates so that you do not encounter version control problems with the templates.

Time Configuration

It is very important that system time is accurate and that all servers are using the same time source. The Windows 2000 W32Time service provides time synchronization for Windows 2000-based computers running in an Active Directory domain. The W32Time service ensures that Windows 2000-based clients' clocks are synchronized with the domain controllers in a domain. This is necessary for Kerberos authentication, but the time synchronization also assists in event log analysis.

The W32Time service synchronizes clocks using the Simple Network Time Protocol (SNTP) as described in RFC 1769. In a Windows 2000 forest, time is synchronized in the following manner:

[handwritten: N.B.]

- The primary domain controller (PDC) emulator operations master in the forest root domain is the authoritative time source for the organization.

- All PDC operations masters in other domains in the forest follow the hierarchy of domains when selecting a PDC emulator with which to synchronize their time.

- All domain controllers in a domain synchronize their time with the PDC emulator operations master in their domain as their in-bound time partner.

- All member servers and client desktop computers use the authenticating domain controller as their in-bound time partner.

[handwritten: ✳] To ensure that the time is accurate, the PDC emulator in the forest root domain should be synchronized to an external SNTP time server. You can configure this by running the following net time command, where <server_list> is your server list:

```
net time /setsntp:<server_list>
```

> **Note:** If your PDC emulator in the forest root is behind a firewall, you may have to open UDP port 123 on the firewall to allow the PDC Emulator to connect to an Internet-based SNTP time server.

If your network uses older Windows operating systems, on these computers, clocks can be synchronized using the following command in a logon script where <timecomputer> is a domain controller on the network:

[handwritten: N T Server]
[handwritten: N T Workstation]

```
net time \\<timecomputer> /set /yes
```

> **Note:** Computers running an operating system other than Windows should also synchronize their clocks to external time sources to allow logging events to be analyzed, based on time. For more information see the Microsoft Knowledge Base article Q216734,"How to Configure an Authoritative Time Server in Windows."

[handwritten diagram and notes: Forest B PDC — GMS — FOREST A — PDC emulation — DC DC DC DC — authing DC — member servers, member clients — Scripts → change, need to synchronise with DC's, not BDC's]

Policy Design and Implementation

If you are going to use Group Policy effectively, you must carefully determine how it will be applied. To simplify the process of applying and checking Group Policy security settings, we recommend that you apply security settings at two levels:

- **Domain Level.** To address the common security requirements, such as account policies and audit policies that must be enforced for all servers.

- **OU Level.** To address specific server security requirements that are not common to all the servers in the network. For example, the security requirements for infrastructure servers differ from those for servers running IIS.

Group Policy settings that affect security are divided into multiple sections.

Table 3.2: Sections of Group Policy and Their Purpose

Policy Section	Description
Account Policy\Password Policy	Password age, length and complexity configured
Account Policy\Account Lockout Policy	Lockout duration, threshold and reset counter configured
Account Policy\Kerberos Policy	Ticket lifetimes configured
Local Policies\Audit Policy	Enable/Disable recording of specific events
Local Policies\User Rights and so on	Define rights such as log on locally, access from network
Local Policies\Security Options	Modify specific security related registry values
Event Log	Success and Failure monitoring enabled
Restricted Groups	Administrators can control who belongs to a specific group
System Services	Controls Startup Mode for each service
Registry	Configure permissions on registry keys
File System	Configure permissions on folders, subfolders and files

All computers have a predefined local policy. When an Active Directory domain is initially created, default domain and domain controller policies are also created. Before you modify any default policies, it is important to document the settings they contain, so that you can easily return to the previous state in the event of a problem.

Handwritten margin notes: HCORIFAP   HCORI EXC   BEORI WEB

Server Roles

Handwritten margin note: COM

For this guide, we have defined several server roles and have created security templates to increase the security for these roles.

Table 3.3: Windows 2000 Server Roles

Server Role	Description	Security Templates
Windows 2000 Domain Controller	An Active Directory domain controller	BaselineDC.inf
Windows 2000 Application Server	A locked down member server on which a service, such as Exchange 2000, can be installed. To allow the service to function correctly, security will have to be loosened.	Baseline.inf
Windows 2000 File and Print Server	A locked down file and print server.	Baseline.inf and File and Print Incremental.inf
Windows 2000 Infrastructure Server	A locked down DNS, Windows Internet Name Service (WINS), and DHCP server.	Baseline.inf and Infrastructure Incremental.inf
Windows 2000 IIS Server	A locked down IIS Server.	Baseline.inf and IIS Incremental.inf

Handwritten margin notes: DC, EXC SQL, FAP, NET, WEB INT, HUB?, COM

The security requirements for each of these roles are different. Appropriate security settings for each role are discussed in detail in Chapter 4, "Securing Servers Based on Role."

Note: This guide assumes that servers perform specific defined roles. If your servers do not match these roles, or you have multipurpose servers, you should use the settings defined here as a guideline for creating your own security templates. However, you should bear in mind that the more functions each of your servers perform, the more vulnerable they are to attack.

Active Directory Structure to Support the Server Roles

As already mentioned, you can apply Group Policy in many different ways, using multiple GPOs and at many different levels of hierarchy. For this guide, we have defined a number of Group Policy settings that you can use to secure the various server roles. You will need to ensure that your Active Directory structure allows you to apply these settings.

To help you secure your Windows 2000-based environment, we have predefined some security templates that can be imported into GPOs. However, if you are going to use these as is, you will need to make sure that you have the appropriate Active Directory structure. The GPOs defined in this guide are designed to be used with the OU structure shown in the diagram.

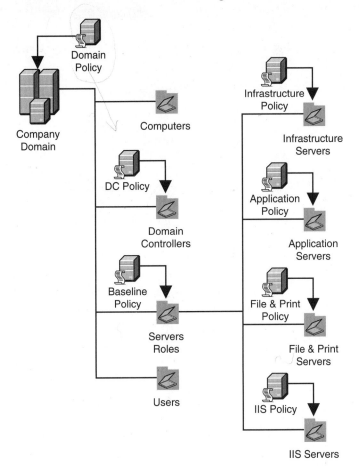

Figure 3.2

OU structure for use with defined GPOs

Note: The domain structure is not important here, as domain and OU Group Policy only apply in the domain in which they were defined. The site structure is also unimportant as we do not define GPOs at the site level in this guide.

▶ **To create the OU structure**

1. Start **Active Directory Users and Computers**.

2. Right-click the domain name, select **New**, and then select **Organizational Unit**.

3. Type **Member Servers** and then click **OK**.

4. Right-click **Member Servers**, select **New**, and then select **Organizational Unit**.

5. Type **Application Servers** and then click **OK**.

6. Repeat steps 5 and 6 for **File & Print Servers**, **IIS Servers**, and **Infrastructure Servers**.

It is worth looking at the OU structure in some more detail.

Domain Level Policy

On cle case, when NT4 PDC is upgraded, old policy is kept.

When a Windows 2000 domain is built, a default domain policy is created. For security settings that you want to apply to the whole domain, you can either:

- Create an additional policy and link it above the default policy
- Modify the existing default policy

Modifying the existing policy is generally simpler, however the advantage of creating an additional domain policy instead of modifying the default policy is that if there are problems with the additional policy, it can be disabled, leaving the default domain policy to resume control.

Remember that domains often contain client computers and users as well as servers. So if you are specifically looking to lock down servers, it will often be impractical to define the specific settings at the domain level. In practice, it is usually best to restrict your server security settings to those that must be set at the domain level.

In this operations guide, we do not define specific settings at the domain level, as many, such as password length, will change according to the overall security policy of your organization. We do however make some general recommendations, which can be found in Chapter 4, "Securing Servers Based on Role."

Note: The password and account policy will ONLY affect domain accounts if they are set at the domain level (which means that you can only configure one password and account policy per domain). If these policies are set at the OU level or anywhere else, they will only affect local accounts. For more information, review the Knowledge Base article Q259576,"Group Policy Application Rules for Domain Controllers."

OK, for us

Member Servers OU

Many of the security settings you define for member servers should apply across every member server role. To simplify this process, we have created a baseline security template called Baseline.inf that you can import into a GPO and apply to the Member Servers OU. These settings will apply both to the Member Servers OU and any child OUs.

Domain Controllers OU

Windows 2000 already comes with a Domain Controllers OU. When a server becomes a domain controller, it is automatically placed here and you should not remove it, as it can cause user log on and access problems.

With this guide, we provide you with a security template called BaselineDC.inf, that you can import into a GPO and apply to the Domain Controller OU. You may choose to apply this in addition to the Default Domain Controllers GPO, or simply modify the settings in the Default Domain Controllers GPO.

Individual Server Role OUs

The individual server role OUs are child OUs to the Member Server OU. This means that by default these servers will all take on the settings defined in your Member Server Baseline Policy.

If you use the baseline policy to secure your member servers, you will need to make alterations which will apply to each individual server role. You can do this by assigning GPOs to each server role OU.

With this guide, we provide security templates that you can import into GPOs for each server role OU. Server roles are discussed in more detail in Chapter 4, "Securing Servers Based on Role."

Importing the Security Templates

The following procedure imports the security templates included with this guide into the OU structure suggested in this chapter. Before implementing the following procedure on a domain controller, you must extract the contents of the SecurityOps.exe file included with this guide.

Warning: The security templates in this guide are designed to increase security in your environment. It is quite possible that by installing the templates included with this guide, you will lose some functionality in your environment. This could include the failure of mission critical applications. It is therefore ESSENTIAL that you thoroughly test these templates before deploying them in a production environment, and make any changes to them that are appropriate for your environment. Back up each domain controller and server prior to applying new security settings. Make sure the system state is included in the backup, because this is where the registry data is kept, and on domain controllers it also includes all of the objects in Active Directory.

Note: Before continuing, if you are using Windows 2000 Service Pack 2, you will need to apply the hot fix discussed in Knowledge Base article Q295444, "SCE Cannot Alter a Service's SACL Entry in the Registry." If this fix is not applied, the Group Policy templates will not be able to disable any services.

► **Importing the Domain Controller Baseline Policy**

1. In **Active Directory Users and Computers**, right-click **Domain Controllers**, and then select **Properties**.

2. On the **Group Policy** tab, click **New** to add a new Group Policy object.

3. Type **BaselineDC Policy** and press **Enter**.

4. Right click **BaselineDC Policy** and select **No Override**.

Note: This is required because the default domain controller policy configures all audit policy settings to No Auditing, with the exception of account management. Because the default domain controller policy has a higher precedence, the No Auditing setting will become the effective setting.

---

5. Click **Edit**.

6. Expand **Windows Settings**, right-click **Security Settings**, and select **Import Policy**.

Note: If Import Policy does not appear on the menu, close the Group Policy window and repeat steps 4 and 5.

---

7. In the **Import Policy From** dialog box, navigate to **C:\SecurityOps\Templates**, and double-click **BaselineDC.inf**.

8. Close **Group Policy** and then click **Close**.

9. Force replication between your domain controllers so that all domain controllers have the policy.   (P.31)   (P. 35)

10. Verify in Event Log that the policy was downloaded successfully and that the server can communicate with the other domain controllers in the domain.

11. Restart each domain controller one at a time to ensure that it reboots successfully.

► **Importing the Member Server policies**

1. In **Active Directory Users and Computers**, right-click **Member Servers**, and then select **Properties**.

2. On the **Group Policy** tab, click **New** to add a new Group Policy object.

3. Type **Baseline Policy** and press **Enter**.

4. Click **Edit**.

5. Expand **Windows Settings**, right-click **Security Settings**, and select **Import Policy**.

Note: If Import Policy does not appear on the menu, close the Group Policy window and repeat steps 4 and 5.

---

6. In the **Import Policy From** dialog box, navigate to **C:\SecurityOps\Templates**, and double-click **Baseline.inf**.

7. Close **Group Policy** and then click **Close**.

8. Repeat steps 1 through 7 using the following OU and security template files:

OU	Security Template
File & Print Servers	File and Print Incremental.inf
IIS Servers	IIS Incremental.inf
Infrastructure Servers	Infrastructure Incremental.inf

9. Force replication between your domain controllers so that all domain controllers have the policy.

10. Move a server for each role into the appropriate OU and on the server download the policy by using the **secedit** command. (P. 31)

11. Verify in Event Log that the policy was downloaded successfully and that the server can communicate with the domain controllers and with other servers in the domain. After successfully testing one server in the OU, move the remaining servers in the OU and then apply security. (otherwise have to wait P.31)

12. Restart each server to ensure that they reboot successfully.

Keeping Group Policy Settings Secure

If you are applying security settings using Group Policy, it is important to ensure that the settings themselves are as secure as possible. This is generally achieved by ensuring that the permissions on both the GPOs and the OUs and domains on which they are applied are set appropriately. The templates included with this guide do not modify the default Active Directory permissions, so you will need to modify these permissions manually.

How? WD?

Group Policy settings defined at higher level containers can potentially be over-written by settings at lower level containers. Using the No Override option on the GPO prevents settings on a higher level container from being overwritten.

Note: Do not set **No Override** on the member server baseline policy. Doing so will prevent the server role policies from enabling the appropriate services and settings.

As well as separating the server roles at the OU level, you should also create separate corresponding administrator roles, assigning them administrative rights over only the corresponding OUs. This ensures that if an attacker manages to gain IIS server admin rights, they do not have access to infrastructure servers and so on.

WB

IIS   → me, GC   F & P → me, GC, WB, GF
PRint Server → NE, GF
Infra → me, GC

Only domain level administrators and above should have the rights to change the membership of an OU. If an OU level administrator can remove a server from that OU, they will be able to change the security settings on those servers.

Once policy has been applied to the servers, your work has not ended. You should check your servers on a regular basis to be sure that:

- The correct policy is applied to the server
- An administrator has not changed a setting in the policy and reduced the level of security on your servers
- Any policy updates or changes have been applied to all servers

Verifying that the settings in the GPO have been applied to your servers as expected will allow you to have confidence that your servers are properly secured. There are several methods that can be used to examine the Group Policy on a server in order to verify the policy is correctly set.

Events in the Event Log

If the policy is downloaded successfully, an Event Log event with the following information appears:

Type: Information

SourceID: SceCli

Event ID: 1704

Message String: Security policy in the Group Policy objects are applied successfully

It may take a few minutes for this message to appear after applying the policy. If you do not receive the successful Event Log message, you need to run **secedit / refreshpolicy machine_policy /enforce** and then restart the server to force the policy download. Check the Event Log again after the restart to verify the successful download of the policy.

Note: If services are set to Disabled in a GPO and the server is rebooted once, the services will typically have restarted before the settings defined in the GPO take effect. If you reboot the server a second time, this will ensure that the services set to Disabled are not started.

Verifying Policy Using Local Security Policy MMC

Another method for verifying that the policy has been applied successfully is to review the effective policy setting on the local server.

▶ **To verify the effective policy settings**

1. Start the **Local Security Policy** MMC.
2. Under **Security Settings**, click **Local Policies**, and then click **Security Options**.

3. In the right pane, view the **Effective Setting** column.

The Effective Setting column should display the settings that are configured in the template for the role of the selected server.

Verifying Policy Using Command Line Tools

There are also two command line tools that can be used to verify policy settings.

Secedit

This tool is included in Windows 2000 and can be used to display differences between the template file and the computer's policy. To compare a template with the current policy on a computer, use the following command line:

```
secedit /analyze /db secedit.sdb /cfg <template name>
```

Note: If you apply the templates included with this guide and then run the above command, an access is denied error will be generated. This is expected due to the additional security applied. A log file will still be generated with the results of the analysis.

Gpresult

The *Windows 2000 Server Resource Kit* (Microsoft Press; ISBN: 1-57231-805-8) includes a tool called GPResult that can be used to display the policies currently applied to a server. To obtain a list of the policies applied to a server, use the following command line:

```
Gpresult /c
```

Note: Gpresult is covered in more detail in the "Troubleshooting Group Policy" section later in this chapter.

Auditing Group Policy

It is possible to audit changes to your Group Policy. Auditing policy changes can be used to keep track of who is changing, or attempting to change, policy settings. Auditing the success and failure of policy changes is enabled in the baseline security templates.

Troubleshooting Group Policy

Even though Group Policy is automatically applied, it is possible that the resulting Group Policy on a server is not as expected, mainly because Group Policy can be configured at multiple levels. This section provides some guidelines that can be used to troubleshoot Group Policy.

Note: If you are having a specific problem with Group Policy not covered in this chapter, be sure to check the Microsoft Knowledge Base. Some key Knowledge Base articles related to Group Policy are detailed in the "More Information" section at the end of this chapter as well as the "Troubleshooting Group Policy" whitepaper.

Resource Kit Tools

GPResult and GpoTool are two *Windows 2000 Server Resource Kit* tools that will help you troubleshoot Group Policy problems.

Note: These tools are also available online, see the "More Information" section at the end of this chapter for details.

GPResult

This tool provides a list of all the GPOs that have been applied to a computer, what domain controller the GPOs came from, and the date and time the GPOs were last applied.

When running GPResult on a server to ensure it has the correct GPOs, use the **/c** switch to display information on computer settings only.

When GPResult is used with the **/c** switch, it provides the following general information:

- Operating System
  - Type (Professional, Server, domain controller)
  - Build number and Service Pack details
  - Whether Terminal Services is installed and, if so, the mode it is using
- Computer Information
  - Computer name and location in Active Directory (if applicable)
  - Domain name and type (Windows NT or Windows 2000)
  - Site name

GPResult with the /c switch also provides the following information about Group Policy:

- The last time policy was applied and the domain controller that applied policy, for the user and computer
- The complete list of applied Group Policy objects and their details, including a summary of the extensions that each Group Policy object contains
- Registry settings that were applied and their details
- Folders that are redirected and their details
- Software management information detailing assigned and published applications
- Disk quota information
- IP Security settings
- Scripts

GpoTool

This command-line tool allows you to check the health of the Group Policy objects on domain controllers including:

- **Check Group Policy object consistency.** The tool reads mandatory and optional directory services properties (version, friendly name, extension GUIDs, and Windows 2000 system volume (SYSVOL) data (Gpt.ini)), compares directory services and SYSVOL version numbers, and performs other consistency checks. Functionality version must be 2 and user/computer version must be greater than 0 if the extensions property contains any GUID.
- **Check Group Policy object replication.** It reads the GPO instances from each domain controller and compares them (selected Group Policy container properties and full recursive compare for Group Policy template).
- **Display information about a particular GPO.** Information includes properties that cannot be accessed through the Group Policy snap-in such as functionality version and extension GUIDs.
- **Browse GPOs.** A command-line option can search policies based on friendly name or GUID. A partial match is also supported for both name and GUID.
- **Preferred domain controllers.** By default, all available domain controllers in the domain will be used; this can be overwritten with the supplied list of domain controllers from the command line.
- **Provide cross-domain support.** A command-line option is available for checking policies in different domains.
- **Run in verbose mode.** If all policies are fine, the tool displays a validation message; in case of errors, information about corrupted policies is printed. A command-line option can turn on verbose information about each policy being processed.

Use the following command line to obtain details of a Group Policy as well as if any errors in the policy are detected:

```
GPOTool /gpo:<gpo name>
```

Group Policy Event Log Errors

Some Group Policy Event Log errors indicate specific problems with your environment. Here are two that will prevent Group Policy from being properly applied:

● On a domain controller, warning event 1202 combined with error event 1000. This generally means that a domain controller has been moved from the Domain Controllers OU to another OU which does not have the Default Domain Controllers GPO linked.

● When an administrator attempts to open one of the default GPOs, the following error is returned:

Failed to open Group Policy Object

You may not have appropriate rights.

Details: Unspecified Error

In the event log, events 1000, 1001 and 1004 appear. This is due to a corrupt registry.pol file. By deleting the registry.pol file under SYSVOL, rebooting and making a change to the server, the errors should disappear.

Summary

Windows 2000 Group Policy is a very useful way to provide consistent settings across your Windows 2000-based environment. To deploy it effectively, you should ensure that you are aware of where GPOs are applied, that all of your servers are receiving the appropriate settings, and that you have defined appropriate security on the GPOs themselves.

More Information

For more information from Symantec on corporate security policies, see:

http://securityresponse.symantec.com/avcenter/security/Content/security.articles /corp.security.policy.html

Microsoft Whitepaper on Group Policy:

http://www.microsoft.com/windows2000/techinfo/howitworks/management/grouppolwp.asp

Microsoft Whitepaper on Troubleshooting Group Policy:

http://www.microsoft.com/Windows2000/techinfo/howitworks/management/gptshoot.asp

Knowledge Base articles on Group Policy Troubleshooting:

http://support.microsoft.com/default.aspx?scid=kb;EN-US;Q250842

http://support.microsoft.com/default.aspx?scid=kb;EN-US;Q216359

Administrative Template File Format:

http://msdn.microsoft.com/library/default.asp?url=/library/en-us/policy/policyref_17hw.asp

Security Descriptor Definition Language:

http://msdn.microsoft.com/library/default.asp?url=/library/en-us/security/accctrl_757p.asp

Additional tools and Group Policy information are available in:

The Windows 2000 Server Resource Kit (Microsoft Press; ISBN: 1-57231-805-8)

or online at:

http://www.microsoft.com/windows2000/techinfo/reskit/default.asp

(baseline)   (incremental)

most secure $\longrightarrow$ less secure

4

Securing Servers Based on Role

In the previous chapter we looked at how Group Policy can be used to define security settings on your servers. In this chapter we get into specifics, looking at baseline policies that can be defined for all member servers and domain controllers in the enterprise and then further modifications you would apply for specific server roles.

This approach allows administrators to lock down their servers using centralized baseline policies, applied consistently across all servers in the enterprise. The baseline policies allow only minimal functionality, but do allow servers to communicate with other computers in the domain and be authenticated against domain controllers. From this more secure state additional incremental policies can be applied, allowing each server to only perform the specific tasks defined by their role. Your risk management strategy will determine whether making these changes is appropriate for your environment.

This operations guide partitions policy implementation in the following way:

- **Domain Wide Policy.** Address common security requirements, such as account policies that must be enforced for all servers and workstations.

- **Domain Controller Policy.** Policies that apply to the Domain Controllers OU. Specifically, the configuration settings impact audit policy, security options, and service configuration.

- **Member Server Baseline Policy.** Common settings for all member servers including audit policies, service configuration, policies that restrict access to the registry, file system, as well as other specific security settings, such as clearing the virtual memory page file on system shut down.

- **Server Role Policy.** Four distinct server roles are defined: application servers, file and print servers, infrastructure servers, and IIS servers. Specific security needs and configurations are described for each role.

This chapter deals with these policies and other settings that should be defined for particular server roles. For more information on how Group Policy is used to apply security settings, see Chapter 3, "Managing Security with Windows 2000 Group Policy."

Domain Policy *- inherited from in-place upgrade of NT4 PDC*

In this operations guide, we do not enforce specific settings at the domain level, as many of these settings, such as password length, will change according to the overall security policy of your organization. It is, however, very important that you define these settings appropriately.

Password Policy

By default, a standard password policy is enforced for all servers in the domain. The table lists the settings for a standard password policy, and recommended minimums for your environment.

Table 4.1 Password Policy Default and Recommended Settings

Policy	Default Setting	Recommended Minimum Setting
Enforce password history	1 password remembered	24 passwords remembered
Maximum password age	42 days	42 days
Minimum password age	0 days	2 days
Minimum password length	0 characters	8 characters
Password must meet complexity requirements	Disabled	Enabled
Store password using reversible encryption for all users in the domain	Disabled	Disabled

Complexity Requirements

When the **Password must meet complexity requirements** setting of Group Policy is enabled, it requires passwords to be at least 6 characters in length (although we recommend you set this to 8 characters). It also requires that passwords contain characters from at least three of these classes:

- English upper case letters   A, B, C, ... Z
- English lower case letters   a, b, c, ... z
- Westernized Arabic numerals   0, 1, 2, ... 9
- Nonalphanumeric characters such as punctuation symbols

Note: A password policy should not only be enforced on servers running Windows 2000, but also on any other devices requiring a password for authentication. Network devices, such as routers and switches, are very susceptible to attack if they are using simple passwords. Attackers may try to gain control of these network devices in order to bypass firewalls.

Account Lockout Policy

An effective account lockout policy will help prevent an attacker from successfully guessing the passwords of your accounts. The table lists the settings for a default account lockout policy and recommended minimums for your environment.

Table 4.2: Account Policy Default and Recommended Settings

Policy	Default Setting	Recommended Minimum Setting
Account Lockout Duration	Not Defined	30 minutes
Account Lockout Threshold	0	5 invalid logon attempts
Reset account lockout after	Not Defined	30 minutes

With the recommended minimums listed here, an account that has five invalid logon attempts within 30 minutes is locked out for 30 minutes (after which it will be reset back to 0 bad attempts and log on can be attempted again). The account can only be activated before the 30 minutes are up if an administrator resets the lockout. To increase the level of security in your organization, you should consider increasing the account lockout duration and decreasing the account lockout threshold.

Note: The password and account policy **must** be set at the domain level. If these policies are set on the OU level or anywhere else in Active Directory, they will affect local accounts and not domain accounts. It is only possible to have one domain account policy, for more information see Knowledge Base article Q255550,"Configuring Account Policies in Active Directory."

Member Server Baseline Policy

Once you have configured settings at the domain level, it is time to define common settings for all your member servers. This is done through a GPO at the Member Server OU, known as a baseline policy. A common GPO automates the process of configuring specific security settings on each server. You will also need to manually apply some additional security settings that cannot be done using group policies.

Baseline Group Policy for Member Servers

The configuration of the baseline policy used in this guide is drawn from the hisecws.inf policy included with server and workstation installs. Some of the areas that hisecws.inf addresses include:

- **Audit Policy.** Determines how auditing is performed on your servers.
- **Security Options.** Determines specific security settings using registry values.
- **Registry Access Control Lists.** Determines who can access the registry.
- **File Access Control Lists.** Determines who can access the file system.
- **Service Configuration.** Determines which services are started, stopped, disabled, and so on.

For this guide we have altered hisecws.inf to make it more secure. The Member Server Baseline Policy, baseline.inf, will help to create a server that is significantly more resistant to attack in production environments.

Hisecws.inf has been altered by adding:

- Registry values pertaining to security
- Service configuration
- Tighter file access control lists
- Enhanced auditing configuration

Member Server Baseline Auditing Policy

The settings for the application, security, and system event logs, are configured in the policy and applied to all member servers in the domain. The size for each of the logs is set at 10 megabyte (MB), and each log is configured to not overwrite events. Therefore, it is important for an administrator to regularly review and archive or clear the logs as appropriate.

Note: If a management system regularly monitors the logs for specific events, and extracts and forwards details to a management database, you will capture the necessary data and therefore can set the log files to overwrite.

The table shows the settings defined in the Member Server Baseline Auditing Policy.

Table 4.3: Member Server Baseline Audit Policy Settings

Policy	Computer Setting
Audit account logon events	Success, Failure
Audit account management	Success, Failure
Audit directory service access	Failure
Audit logon events	Success, Failure
Audit object access	Success, Failure
Audit policy change	Success, Failure
Audit privilege use	Failure
Audit process tracking	No Auditing
Audit system events	Success, Failure
Restrict guest access to the application log	Enabled
Restrict guest access to the security log	Enabled
Restrict guest access to the system log	Enabled
Retention method for application log	Do not overwrite events (clear log manually)
Retention method for security log	Do not overwrite events (clear log manually)
Retention method for system log	Do not overwrite events (clear log manually)
Shut down the computer when the security audit log is full	Not Defined

Note: The retention method policy settings **Manually** is shown, which means do not overwrite events (clear log manually).

Member Server Baseline Security Options Policy

The following security options are configured in the baseline group policy.

Table 4.4: Member Server Baseline Security Options Policy Settings

Option	Setting
Additional restrictions for anonymous connections	No access without explicit anonymous permissions
Allow server operators to schedule tasks (domain controllers only)	Disabled
Allow system to be shut down without having to log on	Disabled
Allowed to eject removable NTFS media	Administrators
Amount of idle time required before disconnecting session	15 minutes
Audit the access of global system objects	Disabled
Audit use of Backup and Restore privilege	Disabled
Automatically log off users when logon time expires	Not Defined (see note)
Automatically log off users when logon time expires (local)	Enabled
Clear virtual memory page file when system shuts down	Enabled
Digitally sign client communication (always)	Enabled
Digitally sign client communication (when possible)	Enabled
Digitally sign server communication (always)	Enabled
Digitally sign server communication (when possible)	Enabled
Disable CTRL+ALT+DEL requirement for logon	Disabled
Do not display last user name in logon screen	Enabled
LAN Manager Authentication Level	Send NTLMv2 responses only, refuse LM & NTLM
Message text for users attempting to log on	
Message title for users attempting to log on	

Option	Setting
Number of previous logons to cache (in case domain controller is not available)	0 logons
Prevent system maintenance of computer account password	Disabled
Prevent users from installing printer drivers	Enabled
Prompt user to change password before expiration	14 days
Recovery Console: Allow automatic administrative logon	Disabled
Recovery Console: Allow floppy copy and access to drives and folders	Disabled
Rename administrator account	Not defined
Rename guest account	Not defined
Restrict CD-ROM drive access to locally logged-on user only	Enabled
Restrict floppy access to locally logged-on user only	Enabled
Secure channel: Digitally encrypt or sign secure channel data (always)	Enabled
Secure channel: Digitally encrypt secure channel data (when possible)	Enabled
Secure channel: Digitally sign secure channel data (when possible)	Enabled
Secure channel: Require strong (Windows 2000 or later) session key	Enabled
Secure system partition (for RISC platforms only)	Not defined
Send unencrypted password to connect to third-party SMB servers	Disabled
Shut down system immediately if unable to log security audits	Enabled (see the second note)
Smart card removal behavior	Lock Workstation
Strengthen default permissions of global system objects (for example, Symbolic Links)	Enabled
Unsigned driver installation behavior	Do not allow installation
Unsigned non-driver installation behavior	Warn but allow installation

Note: The default domain policy configures **Automatically log off users when logon time expires** to disabled. To configure this option you must edit the default domain policy and therefore it is not defined in the baseline policies included with this guide.

Note: If you significantly increase the number of objects you audit, you run the risk of filling the security log and thus forcing a shutdown of the system. The system will then not be usable until an administrator clears the log. To prevent this, you should either disable the shutdown option listed in the table, or preferably, increase the security log size.

Some of the options set here need further discussion as they directly affect the way servers communicate with each other in the domain and can also have an impact on server performance.

Additional Restrictions for Anonymous Connections

By default, Windows 2000 allows anonymous users to perform certain activities such as enumerating the names of domain accounts and network shares. This allows an attacker to view these accounts and share names on a remote server without having to authenticate with a user account. To better secure anonymous access, **No access without explicit anonymous permissions** can be configured. The effect of this is to remove the Everyone group from the anonymous users token. Any anonymous access to a server will not be allowed, and will require explicit access to any resources.

Note: For details on the effect this may have in your environment, see Knowledge Base article Q246261, "How to Use the RestrictAnonymous Registry Value in Windows 2000."

LAN Manager Authentication Level

The Microsoft Windows 9x and Windows NT® operating systems cannot use Kerberos for authentication, and so, by default, they use the NTLM protocol for network authentication in a Windows 2000 domain. You can enforce a more secure authentication protocol for Windows 9x and Windows NT by using NTLMv2. For the logon process, NTLMv2 introduces a secure channel to protect the authentication process.

Note: If you do use NTLMv2 for legacy clients and servers, Windows 2000-based clients and servers will continue to authenticate with Windows 2000 domain controllers using Kerberos. For information on enabling NTLMv2, see Knowledge Base article Q239869, "How to Enable NTLM 2 Authentication for Windows 95/98/2000/NT." Windows NT 4.0 requires service pack 4 to support NTLMv2 and Windows 9x platforms need the directory service client installed in order to support NTLMv2.

Clear Virtual Memory Page File When System Shuts Down

Important information kept in real memory may be dumped periodically to the page file. This helps Windows 2000 handle multitasking functions. If you enable this option, Windows 2000 clears the page file when the system is shut down, removing all information stored there Depending on the size of the page file, it could take several minutes before the system is completely shut down.

Digitally Sign Client/Server Communication

Implementing digital signing in high security networks helps to prevent imperson-ation of clients and servers (known as session hijacking or man in the middle attack). Server message block (SMB) signing authenticates both the user and the server hosting the data. If either side fails the authentication, data transmission will not take place. When SMB signing is implemented, there will be a performance overhead of up to 15 percent in order to sign and verify each packet between the servers. For more information on the performance overhead impact, see Knowledge Base article Q161372, "How to Enable SMB Signing in Windows NT."

Additional Security Options

For this guide, additional registry values were added to the baseline security template file that are not defined within the Administrative Template (ADM) file. This means that when you load the MMC Security Templates snap-in and view the baseline.inf template, the registry values in tables 4.5–4.11 are not represented. Instead, these settings can be added to the .inf file using a text editor and will be applied to the server when the policy is downloaded.

Note: For more information on the relationship between .inf and .adm files, see Knowledge Base article Q228460, "Location of ADM (Administrative Template) Files in Windows."

These settings are embedded within the Baseline.inf security template in order to automate the changes. If the policy is removed, these settings are not automatically removed with it and must be manually changed.

Security Considerations for Network Attacks

Some denial of service attacks can pose a threat to the TCP/IP stack on Windows 2000-based servers. These registry settings help to increase the resistance of the Windows 2000 TCP/IP stack to standard types of denial of service network attacks. Information on these settings can be found in Knowledge Base article Q315669, "HOW TO: Harden the TCP/IP Stack in Windows 2000 Against Denial of Service."

The following registry keys have been added to the template file as subkeys of
HKLM\System\CurrentControlSet\Services\Tcpip I Parameters:

Table 4.5: TCP/IP Parameters Added to the Registry by the Member Server Baseline Policy

Key	Format	Value (Decimal)
EnableICMPRedirect	DWORD	0
EnableSecurityFilters	DWORD	1
SynAttackProtect	DWORD	2
EnableDeadGWDetect	DWORD	0
EnablePMTUDiscovery	DWORD	0
KeepAliveTime	DWORD	300,000
DisableIPSourceRouting	DWORD	2
TcpMaxConnectResponseRetransmissions	DWORD	2
TcpMaxDataRetransmissions	DWORD	3
NoNameReleaseOnDemand	DWORD	1
PerformRouterDiscovery	DWORD	0
TCPMaxPortsExhausted	DWORD	5

Windows Sockets applications such as FTP servers and Web servers have their
connection attempts handled by Afd.sys. Afd.sys has been modified to support
large numbers of connections in the half open state without denying access to
legitimate clients. This is accomplished by allowing the administrator to configure
a dynamic backlog. The new version of Afd.sys supports four new registry parameters that can be used to control the dynamic backlog behavior. For more details on
these settings, see Knowledge Base article Q142641, "Internet Server Unavailable
Because of Malicious SYN Attacks."

The following registry keys have been added to the template file as subkeys of
HKLM\System\CurrentControlSet\Services\AFD\Parameters:

Table 4.6: Afd.sys Settings Added to the Registry by the Member Server Baseline Policy

Key	Format	Value (Decimal)
DynamicBacklogGrowthDelta	DWORD	10
EnableDynamicBacklog	DWORD	1
MinimumDynamicBacklog	DWORD	20
MaximumDynamicBacklog	DWORD	20000

Disable Auto Generation of 8.3 Filenames

Windows 2000 supports 8.3 file name formats for backward compatibility with16-bit applications. This means that an attacker only needs 8 characters to refer to a file that may be 20 characters long. If you avoid using 16-bit applications you can turn this feature off. Disabling short name generation on an NTFS partition also increases directory enumeration performance.

The following registry key has been added to the template as a subkey of **HKLM\System\CurrentControlSet\Control\FileSystem\:**

Table 4.7: Setting to Remove 8.3 Filename Creation Added to the Registry by the Member Server Baseline Policy

Key	Format	Value (Decimal)
NtfsDisable8dot3NameCreation	DWORD	1

Note: If you apply this setting to an existing server that already has files with auto generated 8.3 file names, it does not remove them. To remove existing 8.3 file names, you will need to copy those files off the server, delete the files from the original location, and then copy the files back to their original locations.

Disable Lmhash Creation

Windows 2000-based servers can authenticate computers running all previous versions of Windows. However, previous versions of Windows do not use Kerberos for authentication, so Windows 2000 supports Lan Manager (LM), Windows NT (NTLM) and NTLM version 2 (NTLMv2).The LM)hash is relatively weak compared to the NTLM hash and therefore prone to rapid brute force attack. If you do not have clients that require LM authentication you should disable the storage of LM hashes. Windows 2000 Service Pack 2 provides a registry setting to disable the storage of the LM hashes.

The following registry key has been added to the template as a subkey of **HKLM\SYSTEM\CurrentControlSet\Control\Lsa\:**

Table 4.8: Setting to Disable Lmhash Creation Added to the Registry by Member Server Baseline Policy

Key	Format	Value (Decimal)
NoLMHash	DWORD	1

Note: To disable the storage of LM hashes with this registry setting you must be running Windows 2000 Service Pack 2 or later.

For more information, see the Microsoft Knowledge Base article Q147706, "How to Disable LM Authentication on Windows NT."

Configuring NTLMSSP Security

The NTLM Security Support Provider (NTLMSSP) allows you to specify the minimum required security setting for server side network connections by applications.

The Member Server Baseline Policy ensures that the connection will fail if message confidentiality is in use but 128-bit encryption is not negotiated.

The following registry key has been added to the template as a subkey of **HKLM\SYSTEM\CurrentControlSet\Control\Lsa\MSV1_0**:

Table 4.9: Setting to Configure NTLMSSP Security added to the registry by the Member Server Baseline Policy

Key	Format	Value (Hex)
NtlmMinServerSec	DWORD	0x20000000

Disabling Autorun

Autorun begins reading from a drive as soon as media is inserted in it. As a result, the setup file of programs and the sound on audio media starts immediately. To prevent a possible malicious program from starting when media is inserted the Group Policy disables Autorun on all drives.

The following registry key has been added to the template as a subkey of **HKLM\SOFTWARE\Microsoft\Windows\CurrentVersion\Policies\Explorer**:

Table 4.10: Setting to Disable Autorun on all Drives, Added to the Registry by the Member Server Baseline Policy

Key	Format	Value (Hex)
NoDriveTypeAutoRun	DWORD	0xFF

Member Server Baseline Registry Access Control Lists Policy

The Member Server Baseline Policy does not change the registry ACLs defined in hisecws.inf. You should perform careful testing in your environment before you make any changes.

The ACLs defined in hisecws.inf mainly change the Power Users group, which is created by default for backward compatibility with Windows NT 4.0–based environments. The template ensures that Power Users has the same permissions as the Users group on Windows 2000.

Note: The Power Users group is not defined on domain controllers.

Member Server Baseline File Access Control Lists Policy

To further secure the file system, you should ensure that more restrictive permissions are applied to directories and files common to all member servers in the domain. The Member Server Baseline Security Template incorporates all the file access control lists provided with the hisecws.inf template and adds settings for a number of folders and files.

Note: For details on the default registry and file permissions in Windows 2000, see the "Default Access Control Settings in Windows 2000" white paper available on TechNet. The "More Information" section at the end of this chapter has the link to the white paper.

The table shows the additional folders secured by the Member Server Baseline Policy in addition to those defined by the settings in hisecws.inf.

Table 4.11: Settings to Secure Key Directories Defined in the Member Server Baseline Policy

Folders Secured	Permissions Applied
%systemdrive%\	Administrators: Full control System: Full control Authenticated Users: Read and Execute, List Folder Contents, and Read
%SystemRoot%\Repair %SystemRoot%\Security %SystemRoot%\Temp %SystemRoot%\system32\Config %SystemRoot%\system32\Logfiles	Administrators: Full control Creator/Owner: Full control System: Full control
%systemdrive%\Inetpub	Administrators: Full control System: Full control Everyone: Read and Execute, List Folder Contents, and Read

---

Note: %SystemRoot% defines the path and folder name where the Windows system files are located and %SystemDrive% defines the drive containing %systemroot%.

There are also a large number of files installed on the server that should be locked down further. The Member Server Baseline Policy will alter the ACLs on the default Windows startup files and also on many of the executables that can be run from the command prompt. The files affected are listed in Appendix A.

Member Server Baseline Services Policy

When Windows 2000 Server is first installed, default services are created and are configured to run when the system starts. Some of these services do not need to run in many environments, and as any service is a potential point of attack, you should disable unnecessary services.

The Member Server Baseline Policy only enables the services required for a Windows 2000 member server to participate in a Windows 2000 domain and provide basic management services.

Table 4.12: Services Enabled by the Member Server Baseline Policy

Service	Startup Type	Reason for inclusion in Member Server Baseline
COM+ Event Services	Manual	Allows management of Component Services
DHCP Client	Automatic	Required to update records in Dynamic DNS
Distributed Link Tracking Client	Automatic	Used to maintain links on NTFS volumes
DNS Client	Automatic	Allows resolution of DNS names
Event Log	Automatic	Allows event log messages to be viewed in Event log
Logical Disk Manager to date	Automatic	Required to ensure dynamic disk information is up
Logical Disk Manager Administrative Service	Manual	Required to perform disk administration
Netlogon	Automatic	Required for domain participation
Network Connections	Manual	Required for network communication
Performance Logs and Alerts	Manual	Collects performance data for the computer, writes it to log or triggers alerts
Plug and Play	Automatic	Required for Windows 2000 to identify and use system hardware
Protected Storage	Automatic	Required to protect sensitive data such as private keys
Remote Procedure Call (RPC)	Automatic	Required for internal processes in Windows 2000
Remote Registry Service	Automatic	Required for hfnetchk utility (see Note)
Security Accounts Manager	Automatic	Stores account information for local security accounts
Server	Automatic	Required for hfnetchk utility (see Note)
System Event Notification	Automatic	Required to record entries in the event logs

Service	Startup Type	Reason for inclusion in Member Server Baseline
TCP/IP NetBIOS Helper Service	Automatic	Required for software distribution in Group Policy (may be used to distribute patches)
Windows Management Instrumentation Driver	Manual	Required to implement performance alerts, using Performance Logs and Alerts
Windows Time	Automatic	Required for Kerberos authentication to consistently function
Workstation	Automatic	Required to participate in a domain

Note: Hfnetchk is a tool which allows you to verify which patches are installed on each of the servers in your organization. We recommend the use of this tool in Chapter 5, "Patch Management."

These settings assume a pure and standard Windows 2000-based environment (with the exception of the hfnetchk tool). If your environment involves Windows NT 4.0 (or you have other tools on all your member servers) you may require other services for compatibility purposes. If you do enable other services, these may in turn have dependencies that require further services. Services needed for a specific server role can be added in the policy for that server role.

Appendix B shows all the services present in a default installation of Windows 2000 and Appendix C shows the additional services that may be added to a default installation.

Key Services Not Included in the Member Server Baseline

The goal of the Member Server Baseline Policy is to be as restrictive as possible. For this reason several services are disabled that may be required in your environment. Some of the more common ones are listed here.

SNMP Service

In many cases, management applications require an agent to be installed on each server. Typically, these agents will use SNMP to forward alerts back to a centralized management server. If management agents are required then you should check to see if they need the SNMP service started.

WMI Services

The Windows Management Instrumentation (WMI) service is disabled in the Member Server Baseline Policy. To manage logical disks using computer management, you need to enable the WMI service. Many other applications and tools also use WMI.

Messenger Service and Alert Service

Although not explicitly dependent on one another, these services work together to send administrative alerts. The Messenger service will send alerts triggered by the Alert service. If you are using Performance Logs and Alerts to trigger alerts, you will need to enable these services.

Domain Controller Baseline Policy

All domain controllers created in the domain are automatically assigned to the Domain Controllers OU. Domain controllers should never be moved out of the Domain Controllers OU as there are specific security ACLs applied to this OU.

The Domain Controllers OU is a top level OU and so will not take on the settings defined in your Member Server Baseline Policy. For this reason, we have created a separate Domain Controller Baseline Policy.

Configuration settings implemented in the Domain Controller Baseline Policy affects the following sections of the policy:

- Audit Policy
- Security Options
- Service Configuration

Note: File ACLs, with the exception of the System32 files listed in Appendix A, and registry ACLs are not included in this Group Policy, as they are defined and implemented when the server running Windows 2000 is promoted to a domain controller. A security template called Defltdc.inf is applied during the promotion of a Windows 2000-based server to a domain controller. This template applies ACLs to the file system and registry keys for the additional services created to support a domain controller.

Domain Controller Baseline Audit and Security Options Policy

The audit policy and security options configured for the domain controllers are identical to the baseline policy (see the "Member Server Baseline Policy" section for details on these settings.)

Domain Controller Baseline Services Policy

The services configured for startup are those defined in the member server baseline configuration, plus additional services needed to support the domain controller functions.

Table 4.13: Services Enabled by the Domain Controller Baseline Services Policy, in Addition to Those Set by the Member Server Baseline Policy

Service	Startup Type	Reason for inclusion in Domain Controller Baseline
Distributed File System	Automatic	Required for Active Directory Sysvol share
DNS Server	Automatic	Required for Active Directory integrated DNS
File Replication	Automatic	Needed for file replication between domain controllers
Kerberos Key Distribution Center	Automatic	Allows users to log onto the network using Kerberos v5
NT LM Security Support Provider	Automatic	Allows clients to log on using NTLM authentication
RPC Locator	Automatic	Allows the domain controller to provide RPC name service

Key Services Not Included in the Domain Controller Baseline Policy

The goal of the Domain Controller Baseline Policy is to be as restrictive as possible. For this reason several services are disabled that may be required in your environment. Some of the more common ones you may require are listed here.

Simple Mail Transport Protocol (SMTP)

Intersite replication can occur using either RPC or SMTP. If you use SMTP for replication in your environment, you will need to enable the SMTP Service.

Intersite Messaging

This service is used for mail-based replication between sites. Each transport to be used for replication is defined in a separate add-in dynamic link library (DLL). These add-in DLLs are loaded into Intersite Messaging. Intersite Messaging directs send requests and receive requests to the appropriate transport add-in DLLs, which then route the messages to Intersite Messaging on the destination computer. If you use SMTP for replication in your environment, you will need to enable this service.

IIS Admin Service

If the SMTP service is started then the IIS Admin service also needs to be started as the SMTP service is dependent on the IIS Admin service.

Distributed Link Tracking Server Service

This service is used to track files on NTFS volumes throughout a domain and is contacted by computers running the Distributed Link Tracking Client service. These computers will periodically continue to attempt to contact the Distributed Link Tracking Server service even after it is disabled.

Note: If you run the dcdiag utility from the Windows 2000 Support Tools, it will check for all services which normally run on domain controllers to be started. As some services are disabled in the Domain Controller Baseline Policy, dcdiag will report errors. This is to be expected and does not indicate a problem with your configuration.

Other Baseline Security Tasks

It is not possible to perform all the tasks required to increase the security of your member servers and domain controllers using Group Policy. There are a number of additional steps you should take to increase the overall level of security on all of your servers.

Securing Built-in Accounts

Windows 2000 has a number of built-in user accounts, which cannot be deleted, but can be renamed. Two of the most commonly known built-in accounts on Windows 2000 are Guest and Administrator. By default, the Guest account is disabled on member servers and domain controllers. You should not change this setting. The built-in Administrator account should be renamed and the description altered to prevent attackers from compromising a remote server using a well known name. Many malicious scripts use the built-in administrator account as a first attempt for comprising the server.

Note: The built-in administrator account can be renamed using Group Policy. We have not implemented this setting in the baseline policies because you should choose a name which is not well known.

Securing Local Administrator Account

Every member server has a local accounts database and a local administrator account that provides full control over the server. This account is therefore very important. You should rename this account, and ensure that it has a complex password. You should also ensure that local administrator passwords are not replicated across member servers. If they are, an attacker who gains access to one member server will be able to gain access to all others with the same password.

You should not make local administrator accounts part of the Domain Admins group as this extends their capabilities beyond what is necessary to administer member servers. For the same reason, it is important to ensure that only local accounts are used to administer your member servers.

Securing Service Accounts

Windows 2000 services typically run under the Local System account, but they can also be run under a domain user or local account. You should use local accounts whenever possible over domain user accounts. A service runs under the security context of its service account, so if an attacker compromises a service on a member server, the service account can potentially be used to attack a domain controller. When determining which account to use as a service account, you should make sure that the assigned privileges are limited to what is required for the successful operation of the service. The table below explains the privileges inherent to each type of service account.

Table 4.14: Privileges of Windows 2000 Accounts in Different Environments

Authentication when running service on Windows 2000-based computers	Intraforest only, all Windows 2000-based servers	Multiforest application with NTLM trusts between domains
Local user service account	No network resources, local local access only under account's assigned privileges	No network resources, local access only under account's assigned privileges
Domain user service account	Network access as domain user, local access under user's privileges	Network access as domain user, local access under user's privileges
LocalSystem	Network access as machine account authenticated user, local access under LocalSystem	No network resources spanning forests, local access under LocalSystem

All Windows 2000 default services run under **LocalSystem** and you should not change this. Any additional services added to the system requiring the use of domain accounts should be evaluated carefully before they are deployed.

Validating the Baseline Configuration

After security has been applied for the first time to a server, it is good practice to validate that the specific security settings have been configured correctly. The Microsoft Security Baseline Analyzer Tool will perform a series of tests against your servers, and warn you of any security problems you may encounter.

Validate Port Configuration

It is important to validate the final port configuration and to understand which TCP and UDP ports your servers running Windows 2000 are listening on. After applying the baseline policies, the netstat command can be run to show what ports the server is still listening on for each network interface card. The table shows the expected output netstat for a member server with the Member Server Baseline Policy applied:

Table 4.15: Ports a Member Server Will Listen on After the Member Server Baseline Policy is Applied

Protocol	Local Address	Foreign Address	Status
TCP	0.0.0.0:135	0.0.0.0:0	LISTENING
TCP	0.0.0.0:445	0.0.0.0:0	LISTENING
TCP	<IP Address>:139	0.0.0.0:0	LISTENING
UDP	<IP Address>:137	*.*	N/A
UDP	<IP Address>:138	*.*	N/A
UDP	0.0.0.0:445	*.*	N/A
UDP	0.0.0.0:1027	*.*	N/A
UDP	0.0.0.0:1045	*.*	N/A

Securing Each Server Role

Once you have applied your baseline policies, your servers will be significantly more secure From this state, you may need to enable additional settings, adding functionality to your baseline. For this guide we have defined four distinct member server roles:

- **Windows 2000 Application Server.** The most secure and locked down of the server roles. The goal of the secure application server role is to provide a very locked down server on which you can install an application, such as Exchange or SQL. This server role is designed so that all it can do is communicate with domain controllers for authentication purposes. This role is the basis for the other roles.

- **Windows 2000 File and Print Server.** Designed to greatly increase the security of servers acting as file and print servers.

- **Windows 2000 Infrastructure Server.** Designed to greatly increase the security of servers acting as DNS, DHCP, and WINS servers.

- **Windows 2000 IIS Server.** Designed to greatly increase the security of servers acting as IIS servers. This role uses a modified version of the application server policy as well as using the IIS Lockdown and URLScan tools.

Note: The application server role is deliberately very restricted. In order to install and run certain applications you may well have to alter the security settings from what is defined here.

Note: It is possible to modify the templates included with this guide to build templates for other roles. If this is done, it is important to fully test the modified template to ensure it provides the level of security desired.

Windows 2000 Application Server Role

Settings for the Application Server role will depend on the particular application you are deploying. For this reason, the settings are unchanged from the member server baseline. Therefore the application server role is very restricted—to install and run certain applications you will need to alter the security settings from the defaults defined here. The easiest way to accomplish this, is to create a new OU for the application under the Application Servers OU. Then create a Group Policy that modifies the baseline settings and import the policy into the new OU.

Windows 2000 File and Print Server Role

File and print services are generally accessed and used by all users in a corporate environment, so ensuring that this server role is as secure as possible can be very challenging. The File and Print Server Policy:

- Enables the Spooler service, which is used for printing.
- Disables the security policy setting: **Digitally sign client communication (always)**. If this is not disabled, clients will be able to print, but not able to view the print queue. When attempting to view the print queue they will receive the message: "Unable to connect. Access denied."

Note: The Spooler service is used on any computer that initiates a print job, as well as print servers. The default settings for the member server and domain controller baselines mean that you will not be able to issue print jobs from these computers.

Windows 2000 Infrastructure Server Role

The Infrastructure Server role supports DNS, DHCP and WINS network services. For all three services to execute on one member server, the infrastructure policy enables the following services in addition to the Member Server Baseline Policy.

Table 4.16: Services Added by the Infrastructure Server Role Policy

Service	Startup Type	Reason for inclusion in Infrastructure Server Role Policy
DHCPServer	Automatic	To provide DHCP services to clients
DNS	Automatic	To provide DNS services to clients
NTLMSSP	Automatic	To provide security to RPC programs that use transports other than named pipes
WINS	Automatic	To provide WINS services clients

Windows 2000 IIS Server Role

The IIS server role provides Web server functionality to a Windows 2000-based server. The IIS server role Group Policy adds following services to the Member Server Baseline Policy.

Table 4.16: Services added by the IIS Server Role Policy

Service	Startup Type	Reason for inclusion in IIS Server Role Policy
IISAdmin	Automatic	Administration of the Web Server
W3SVC	Automatic	Provides Web Server Functionality

In addition, the IIS server role Group Policy configures the **SynAttackProtect** registry value to 1.

The IISLockdown tool

IIS servers provide a great deal of functionality. However, to make your IIS servers as secure as possible, you should restrict this functionality to only that which is required. The easiest way to do this is with the IISLockdown tool. IISLockdown is a highly configurable utility that allows you to specify the nature of your Web server. It will then remove any functionality that is not required for the particular Web server. You should, of course, test thoroughly any changes before implementing them in a production environment.

Note: IISLockdown is available as part of the Security Toolkit and on the Microsoft Security Website. Further details can be found in the "More Information" section at the end of this chapter.

IISLockdown can perform many steps to help secure web servers. These can include:
- Locking files
- Disabling services and components
- Installing URL Scan
- Removing unneeded Internet Server Application Programming Interface (ISAPI) DLL script mappings
- Removing unneeded directories
- Changing ACLs

You can use IIS Lockdown to secure many types of IIS server role. For each server, you should pick the most restrictive role that meets the needs of your Web server.

▶ **To secure a Static Web Server with IIS Lockdown**

1. Start **IISLockd.exe**.
2. Click **Next**.
3. Select **I agree**, and then click **Next**.
4. Select **Static Web server**, and then click **Next**.
5. Ensure **Install URLScan filter on the server** is selected and then **Next**.
6. Click **Next**.
7. If the **Digital Signature Not Found** dialog box appears, click **Yes**.
8. Click **Next**.
9. Click **Finish**.

If you set up IIS Server as a Static Web Server, the following changes are made:

- The Index Server Web Interface (.idq, .htw, .ida) script map is disabled
- The Internet Data Connector (.idc) script map is disabled
- The Server side includes (.shtml, .shtm, .stm) script map is disabled
- The .HTR scripting (.htr)' script map is disabled
- The Active Server Pages (.asp) script map is disabled
- The Internet printing (.printer) script map is disabled
- The printer virtual directory is removed
- Web Distributed Authoring and Versioning (WebDAV) is disabled
- File permissions are set to prevent anonymous IIS users from writing to content directories
- File permissions are set to prevent anonymous IIS users from running system utilities
- The URLScan filter is installed on the server
- The Scripts virtual directory is removed
- The MSADC virtual directory is removed
- The IIS Samples virtual directory is removed
- The IISAdmin virtual directory is removed
- The IISHelp virtual directory is removed

Note: More information on URLScan can be found in Chapter 6, "Auditing and Intrusion Detection."

Other IIS Server Role Security Settings

The IIS Lockdown tool significantly increases the security of your IIS servers. However, there are further steps you can take to further secure your servers running Windows 2000 IIS service.

Setting IP Address/DNS Address Restrictions

This setting ensures that only systems with particular IP addresses or DNS names can access the web server. Setting IP address and DNS address restrictions is not typically done, but it is one option available to restrict Web sites to certain users. However, if DNS names are used instead of IP addresses in the restrictions, IIS has to do a DNS lookup, which can be time consuming.

Disabling the Default IIS Anonymous Account

On Member Servers running IIS, the default anonymous account used to access IIS is a local account, named **IUSR_computername**. For additional security, you should consider disabling the default account and replacing it with another local account, adhering to strong password guidelines. This will make it more difficult for an attacker to guess the name of the account.

Note: You can delete the **IUSR_computername** account, however disabling the account instead leaves it as a decoy account.

Implementing IPSec Filters for Multihomed Web Servers

The IPSec policy engine that comes with Windows 2000 is a useful tool to increasing the overall security of your Web architecture, particularly the security of your Web servers. The IPSec policy is usually used to create a secure communication path between two host sites or two remote sites. However, it can also be used for its protocol/port filtering capabilities.

You can use filter lists in conjunction with filter actions to control the traffic to and from your Web server. For example, you could create two filter lists, one for traffic from all destinations coming to Port 80, another for traffic from all destinations to all ports. You would then define filter actions to allow the traffic matching the first filter list through and to block traffic matching the second filter list.

IPSec policies are implemented using Group Policy. We have not incorporated them in the policies included in this guide, as they will be implemented differently according to the specifics of your environment.

Changes to the Recommended Environment

The goal of the recommendations listed in this chapter is to create a significantly more secure environment for Windows 2000-based servers. However, some of the changes may not be appropriate for your organization. Here we look at two cases where 1) more administrative capability is required, and 2) where the Hfnetchk utility will not be used.

Administration Changes

The default baseline polices for member servers and domain controllers will eliminate some of the remote (and some of the local) administrative functionality from your environment. Remote management using the Microsoft Management Console (MMC) computer management snap-in will not work with the default baseline policies because some MMC related services are disabled.

The baseline policies enable the Server service and Remote Registry service. This will allow the computer management snap-in to remotely connect to other computers and administer these elements:

- Shared Folders
- Local users and groups
- Under Storage Management, everything except Logical Drives and Removable Storage
- Services Device Manager
- Event Viewer
- Performance Logs and Alerts

WMI is not enabled in the baseline policies. This prevents these elements from being administered:

- WMI
- Under Storage Management, Logical Drives

If you need to administer these, locally or remotely, you should enable the WMI service.

Removable Storage cannot be accessed remotely with just the Member Server Baseline Policy services started. If the Removable Storage service is not started on the remote server then the remote server will produce a DCOM error message in the event log stating that the service is not available.

Note: When enabling the above services to allow administration, enable the services only in the incremental server role policies that require the services.

Note: Some administration tools may require you to make security modifications on the client from which you are running the tool. For example, some tools may use NTLM authentication and the baseline policy configures the servers to only accept NTLM v2. See the "LAN Manager Authentication Level" section in this chapter for more information on configuring this.

Security Modifications if HFNETCHK is Not Implemented

Hfnetchk is a tool which allows you to verify which patches are installed on each of the servers in your organization. We highly recommend that you use a tool such as Hfnetchk as it will help you increase the overall level of security in your environment.

However, if you do not implement Hfnetchk, you can disable the Remote Registry service and Server service in the Member Server Baseline Policy. In the Domain Controller Baseline policy you can disable the Remote Registry service.

If you do disable these services in the Member Server Baseline Policy, you will need to enable them in some of the server roles:

Table 4.17: Services that Must be Added to Server Role GPOs if Remote Registry and Server Services are Disabled in the Member Server Baseline Policy

Server Role	Service to be Enabled	Reason
File and Print Server	Server	To provide File sharing capabilities
Infrastructure Server	Server	To allow WINS to function properly
Infrastructure Server	Remote Registry	To allow the WINS Manager to view the state of the WINS Server

If you do disable the Server and Remote Registry services, you will also lose almost all of your remote administration capabilities.

Summary

Windows 2000-based servers provide a great deal of functionality out of the box. However, much of this functionality is not required for all servers. By defining the tasks that your servers perform, you can disable those elements you do not require, and therefore increase the security in your environment. If you implement the steps suggested in this chapter, you will go a long way toward making your environment significantly more secure.

More Information

For more information from Symantec on the fundamentals of security, see: *http://securityresponse.symantec.com/avcenter/security/Content/security.articles/fundamentals.of.info.security.html*

Information on securing the Windows 2000 TCP/IP Stack:

http://www.microsoft.com/technet/treeview/default.asp?url=/TechNet/security/website/dosrv.asp

Default Access Control Settings in Windows 2000 white paper:

http://www.microsoft.com/technet/treeview/default.asp?url=/TechNet/prodtechnol/windows2000serv/maintain/featusability/secdefs.asp

Microsoft Security Toolkit:

http://www.microsoft.com/security/mstpp.asp

Glossary of Windows 2000 Services:

http://www.microsoft.com/windows2000/techinfo/howitworks/management/w2kservices.asp

5

Patch Management

Operating systems and applications are often immensely complex. They can consist of millions of lines of code, written by many different programmers. It is essential that the software works reliably and does not compromise the security or stability of your IT environment. To minimize any problems, programs are tested thoroughly before release. However, attackers continually strive to find weaknesses in software and anticipating all attacks in the future is impossible.

Software companies release patches to resolve weaknesses, in code or implementation, which become apparent after the release of the product. Increasingly, these problems are security related, as the number of attackers increase, as their methods become more sophisticated, and as new malicious code is created to take advantage of security holes. However, they can also be simply related to adding functionality to the product that is desirable.

Security patches present a specific challenge to most organizations. Once a weakness has been exposed in software, attackers will generally spread information about it quickly throughout the community. Software companies therefore strive to release a security patch as soon as possible. Until you deploy the patch, the security you depend upon and expect may be severely diminished.

Whether your company has thousands of computers or just a few, managing all available patches, determining which are relevant to your environment, and evaluating how much testing you can afford to do before deploying them, can be a difficult and time consuming task.

This chapter is designed to help you keep your Windows 2000-based servers secure, but the processes described in here can also be applied to your patch management processes for all software updates. You should contact the specific manufacturer for details of how they do updates to their software.

Terminology

In this guide we use the terms patch, service pack and hotfix interchangeably to mean changes to the software after its release. This is because the process for deploying them is the same in each case. However, each does have a more specific definition:

Service Packs

Service packs keep the product current, correct known problems, and may also extend your computer's functionality. They include tools, drivers, and updates, including enhancements developed after the product released. They are conveniently packaged for easy downloading.

Service packs are product specific, so there are separate service packs for each product. However, the same service back will generally be used for different versions of the same product. For example, the same service pack is used to update Windows 2000 Server and Windows 2000 Professional.

Service packs are also cumulative—each new service pack contains all the fixes in previous service packs, as well as any new fixes and system modifications that have been recommended since. You do not need to install a previous service pack before you install the latest one.

Hotfixes or QFEs

Quick Fix Engineering (QFE) is a group within Microsoft that produces hotfixes—code patches for products. These are provided to individual customers when they experience critical problems for which no feasible workaround is available. Occasionally you will see technical documentation refer to hotfixes as QFEs.

Hotfixes do not undergo extensive regression testing and are very issue specific—you should apply one only if you experience the exact issue it addresses and are using the current software version with the latest service pack.

Groups of hotfixes are periodically incorporated into service packs, at which time they undergo more rigorous testing, and are made available to all customers.

Security Patches

Security patches are designed to eliminate security vulnerabilities. Attackers wanting to break into systems can exploit these vulnerabilities. These are analogous to hotfixes but are deemed mandatory, if the circumstances match, and need to be deployed quickly.

Many security updates released are for client-side (often browser) issues. They may or may not be relevant to a server installation. You need to obtain the client patch to update your current client base and the admin patch to update the client build area on your server.

Patch Management in Your Organization

Exactly how you implement patch management will depend a great deal on the size and complexity of your organization. However, it is vital that you understand the importance of patch management and how it fits into the overall risk management strategy for your company. For example, if you decide that risk must be minimized at all costs, you could follow a strategy of shutting down all production systems every time a new vulnerability appears in your software. You may then choose to not start the systems again until extensive testing has been done on the security patch and it has been deployed throughout your organization. This is a very time consuming and expensive process and will be completely impractical for many organizations.

Throughout the patch management process, you will need to evaluate the risks against the costs of deploying the appropriate countermeasures. After a security vulnerability has been disclosed, there may be a short period before a patch is released. You will need to evaluate the increased risk caused by the vulnerability and determine the measures to take prior to testing and deployment of a patch. These measures may include disabling services, taking systems offline, or restricting access to internal users or other groups as necessary. Once a patch is released you need to determine the risk of deploying it immediately against the costs of keeping services down or unprotected for a short time while you test and make sure the patch does not affect the system negatively. If you do decide to test, you need to determine how much testing you can afford to do before the risks of not deploying outweigh the risks of deploying.

Note: Your organization should implement a change management process. MOF includes a change management process that can be the foundation for your organization's process. See the link to the MOF in the "More Information" section at the end of this chapter.

Assessing Your Current Environment

Often, patches are applied inconsistently throughout an organization, and there is no documentation on why, when, and where they have been deployed. Before you can manage the security of your environment properly you must know in detail its current state. At a minimum for patch management purposes, you must know:

- What systems are in your environment?
  - OS, including version
  - Patch level (Service Pack version, Hotfixes, and other modifications)
  - Function
  - Applications
  - Ownership and contact information

- What assets are present in your environment and what is their relative value?
- What are the known threats and what process do you have for identifying new ones or changes in threat level?
- What are the known vulnerabilities and what process do you have for identifying new ones or changes in vulnerability level?
- What countermeasures have been deployed?

It is highly recommended that you keep this information available to all those involved in your patch management process, and ensure it remains up to date.

Once you know your assets, vulnerabilities, threats, and how your environment is configured, you can determine which of the threats and vulnerabilities are going to be of concern to your company.

Security Update Systems

In many environments it can be beneficial to have specialized computers from which you perform many of the steps of the patch management process. These systems provide specialized locations for storing security tools, patches, hotfixes, service packs, and documentation. You can use these systems as a place to perform patch analysis, retrieval, and deployment. In this guide, we refer to such systems as Security Update Systems.

You should ensure that your Security Update Systems are on one or more dedicated computers that can be tightly controlled and secured, as these systems will be used for deploying and maintaining security patches for all systems in your environment. Security Update Systems do not generally need to be high powered servers, as the load on them will typically be very light. However, high availability is very important, as these computers will form the basis of keeping your environment up to date with the latest patches.

In order to properly deploy a Security Update System, the computer will need direct or indirect Internet access to download the latest patch information from trusted sources, as well as access to each computer it is responsible for keeping current.

Later in this chapter we will be using examples and sample scripts that should be run from a Security Update System.

Note: MOF discusses update systems as part of the release management process.

Communication

If your company is small, then only one person may need to be put in charge of keeping patches up to date, testing patches, installing patches and reading the various log files. However, in larger environments there will generally be several people in charge of different aspects of security. It is very important that all those involved in patch management communicate effectively. This will help ensure that decisions are made without duplicating effort, and that no steps of the process are missed.

Patch Management and Change Management

Patch management is really just a subset of change management. If you already have a change management procedure in your organization, you will not have to create an entirely new process for patch management. However, it is still worth reading this chapter for information specific to the patch management process.

A good change control procedure has an identified owner, a path for customer input, an audit trail for any changes, a clear announcement and review period, testing procedures, and a well understood back out plan.

Microsoft Security Tool Kit

The Microsoft Security Tool Kit can be useful when it comes to obtaining the service packs and hotfixes needed to keep your servers current. It contains important security information, current service packs, critical security patches for Windows NT 4.0, Windows 2000, IIS, and Internet Explorer. It also includes the Critical Update notification tool. This tool ties back to the Windows Update site to ensure that all the latest patches are installed. The Security Toolkit is available from TechNet.

Patch Management Processes

The patch management process is represented by the flowchart shown in Figure 5.1.

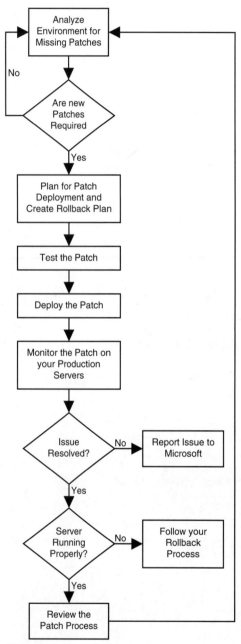

Figure 5.1
Patch management process

It is worth examining these steps in more detail:

- **Analyze.** Look at the current environment and potential threats. Determine the patches you must deploy to reduce the threats to your environment.

- **Plan.** Determine which patches should be deployed to deter the potential threats and vulnerabilities you have identified. Identify who will perform testing and deployment and the steps involved.

- **Testing.** Review the available patches and categorize them for your environment, test all patches that have been identified to make sure they will work within your environment without any negative side effects. Understand what the patch does and how it affects your environment. Verify that it performs as planned.

- **Deploy.** Deploy the right patches to make your environment secure.

- **Monitor.** Check all systems after deploying patches to make sure there are no undesired side effects.

- **Review.** As part of the ongoing process you need to routinely review new patches that have been released, your environment, and which patches are needed for your company. If during the review you find new patches are needed, start again at the first step.

Note: It is highly recommended that you back up all production systems prior to deploying patches.

Analyze Your Environment for Missing Patches

As an ongoing process, you need to ensure that you are up to date on patches. In some cases a new patch will be released and you will need to install it on all servers. In others, a new server will be brought online and will need to be patched appropriately. You should continue to analyze all of your servers to ensure that they are completely current on the latest patches needed. There are a number of tools you can use to help you with this.

Microsoft Network Security Hotfix Checker (Hfnetchk)

Hfnetchk is a command line utility that allows you to check if the current configuration on your servers is up to date and has all the appropriate security patches. This tool works by downloading an Extensible Markup Language (XML) database directly from Microsoft that contains a list of the latest hotfixes to check for in order to stay secure. Hfnetchk will also use a local XML database if you do not have a connection to the Internet, although this could provide out of date results.

Note: To use Hfnetchk, you must have administrator access to the computer being checked for patches, either local administrator or domain administrator.

The tool has a number of command line switches, listed in the following table.

Table 5.1: Hfnetchk Switches

Hfnetchk switch	Function
-about	About hfnetchk.
-h <hostname>	Specifies the NetBIOS machine name to scan. Default is the localhost.
-fh <hostfile>	Specifies the name of a file containing the NetBIOS machine names to scan. One name per line, 256 max per file.
-i <ipaddress>	Specifies the IP address of a machine to scan.
-fip <ipfile>	Specifies the name of a file containing addresses to scan. One IP address per line, 256 max per file..
-r <range>	Specifies the IP address range to be scanned, starting with ipaddress1 and ending with ipaddress2. The range is inclusive.
-d >domain_name>	Specifies the domain name to scan. All machines in the domain will be scanned.
-n <network>	All systems on the local network will be scanned (all hosts in Network Neighborhood).
-history <level>	Not necessary for normal operation.
-t <threads>	Number of threads used for executing scan. Possible values are from 1 to 128. Default is 64
-o <output>	Specifies the desired output format. (tab) outputs in tab delimited format. (wrap) outputs in a word wrapped format. The default is wrap.
-x <datasource>	Specifies the xml datasource containing the hotfix information. Location may be an xmlfilename, compressed xml cab file, or a URL. The default is mssecure.cab from the Microsoft website.
-s <suppress>	Suppresses NOTE and WARNING messages. 1 = Suppress NOTE messages only, 2 = Suppress both NOTE and WARNING messages. The default is to show all messages
-z	Do not perform registry checks.
-nosum	Do not evaluate file checksum. The checksum test calculates the checksum of files. This can use up large amounts of bandwidth. Using this option will speed up a scan and use less bandwidth. File version checks will be still done.
-b	Display the status of hotfixes required to meet minimum baseline security standards.
-v	Displays the details for Patch NOT Found, WARNING and NOTE messages. Enabled by default in tab mode.
-f <outfile>	Specifies name of the file to save the results. Default is to display to screen.
-u <username>	Specifies optional user name for log in to remote computer.

Hfnetchk switch	Function
-p <password>	Specifies password to be used with user name.
-?	Displays a help menu.

If you are using Hfnetchk to verify your patch status, you should ensure that it is run regularly. In most environments, the best way to do this is to schedule it to run regularly.

Note: For more information on the use of Hfnetchk, see the Knowledge Base article Q303215, "Microsoft Network Security Hotfix Checker (Hfnetchk.exe) Tool Is Available."

Patch Management Script

This guide includes a patch management script, hfnetchk.cmd, that will check multiple servers for missing patches and record the results to a log file which is saved in a date-based folder. The script uses Hfnetchk to scan servers, and another script, movelog.vbs, to move the files into the appropriate folders. Over time these folders make up a history that you can review as part of your analysis and review phases, helping you to keep your environment more secure.

Note: The script included with this guide requires Hfnetchk.exe version 3.32 or later.

After downloading and extracting the scripts included with this guide, you will have the following folder structure for the patch management script.

Table 5.2: Folder Structure for the Patch Management Script

Folder	Description
C:\SecurityOps	This is the root folder for all of the files included with this guide.
C:\SecurityOps\PatchMgmt	This folder contains the patch management script, hfnetchk.cmd, the movelog.vbs script, and the sub-folders for the support files and logs. This folder is also where the mssecure.xml file must be placed.
C:\SecurityOps\PatchMgmt\Hfnetchk	This folder is where the hfnetchk.exe utility must be placed after being downloaded from the Microsoft website. See below for more detailed instructions.
C:\SecurityOps\PatchMgmt\ServerLists	This folder is where you create and keep text files listing groups of servers to be scanned for missing patches.
C:\SecurityOps\PatchMgmt\Logs	This folder is where the log files are created after hfnetchk.cmd is run. The script creates a subfolder with the current date in which the log file is stored, for example \SecurityOps\PatchMgmt\Logs \2002117.

> **Note:** If you install the files included with this guide on a partition other than C:, you will need to edit the paths in the hfnetchk.cmd file to use that partition.

▶ To setup and use the Hfnetchk.cmd script on a Security Update System

1. Run SecurityOps.exe to extract the script files included with this guide to create the folder structure listed in table 5.2.

2. Download and extract the Hfnetchk utility from http://www.microsoft.com/Downloads/Release.asp?ReleaseID=31154 and place hfnetchk.exe in the C:\SecurityOps\PatchMgmt\Hfnetchk folder. If the computer that is running the script is not connected to the Internet, you will also need to download and extract the Mssecure.xml file from http://download.microsoft.com/download/xml/security/1.0/nt5/en-us/mssecure.cab. Mssecure.xml should be placed in the C:\SecurityOps\PatchMgmt folder.

3. Create a server list text file in C:\SecurityOps\PatchMgmt\ServerLists. This is a text files containing the NetBIOS names of the servers you want to check, separated by carriage returns.

> **Note:** Hfnetchk.exe version 3.32 will not scan a server if there is a space after the server name and before the carriage return. Before running Hfnetchk, verify that each line does not end with a space.

4. Start a Command Prompt, change to the C:\SecurityOps\PatchMgmt folder, and start the script using the following command line.

   ```
   Hfnetchk.cmd serverlist.txt
   ```

   Where serverlist.txt is the name of the server list text file.

> **Note:** If you receive a dialog box asking is you want to download the mssecure.xml file, click **Yes**.

5. Change to the C:\SecurityOps\PatchMgmt\Logs folder, open the folder with the current date, and open the file with the same name as the serverlist.txt file.

6. Examine the log file to determine what patches are missing on your servers.

> **Note:** If the patch management script is run twice in a single day, the log file from the first time the script was run will be overwritten.

Working with Multiple Server Lists

In a large scale network you will have many different server types. As part of your risk management process you may determine that you need to monitor some of your servers more often than others for missing patches. If you use multiple server lists, you can schedule the patch management script to scan different types of servers at different intervals. Multiple server lists are also useful if you have different administrators responsible for different groups of servers. Using multiple lists, you will be able to create separate reports of missing patches for each group of administrators.

As an example, for the simple network shown in figure 5.2, you could create six server list files to provide patch reports to different groups of administrators.

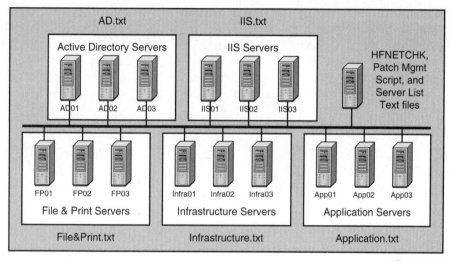

Servers.txt

Figure 5.2
Server list files for a simple network

In this example, the server list files for each type of server would contain the names of those servers. For example, File&Print.txt simply contains:

```
FP01
FP02
FP03
```

The sixth server list file, Servers.txt, contains all of the servers in the environment. The results of this scan could be used by the security team to ensure that each group is keeping their servers up to date with the latest patches.

Scheduling the Patch Management Script

To ensure that hfnetchk.cmd runs regularly, you should consider scheduling the tool to run regularly. This could be done using the task scheduler or the AT command. By using multiple server lists, you could ensure that different servers are checked at different times.

Note: By default, the schedule service is disabled in the Member Server and Domain Controller Baseline Policies. You will need to enable the service if you want to schedule the Patch Management Script.

Other Methods for Determining Hotfix Levels

If you do not want or are unable to use the hfnetchk tool in some parts of your environment, there are other ways you can determine whether hotfixes have been installed.

The easiest way is to look in the registry under the **HKLM\Software\Microsoft\Windows Nt\Currentversion\hotfix** key. Every new hotfix installed should have a key with a Q name which corresponds to the article in the Knowledge Base discussing the hotfix. However, this is not the case for some older hotfixes and hotfixes for some applications.

There are two other free tools from Microsoft that that can be used to gather this information. These tools are:

- **Qfecheck.exe /v.** Tells you the service pack level and hotfixes installed. Qfecheck will also tell you if the patch was not correctly installed.
- **Hotfix.exe -l.** Displays the hotfixes installed.

Plan

Not every threat or vulnerability poses a significant risk to your environment. As you read notifications of potential new operating system or application vulnerabilities, you should assess whether these vulnerabilities apply to your environment. For example, if the vulnerability applies to the FTP service in Windows 2000 and you never enable this service, then the vulnerability does not apply to you. Likewise, if you learn that there is an increased chance of hurricanes this year, but your IT environment is significantly inland, then threat is very minimal. If you respond to threats and vulnerabilities which are not real for your environment, you will use up valuable resources and potentially adversely affect the stability of your environment with no corresponding benefit.

As new threats and vulnerabilities emerge, you should read any supporting information about them. This will allow you to make an intelligent decision as to whether there is significant risk to your environment and therefore determine the appropriate response. This may be to take no action, to disable the service at risk, or to deploy a patch.

Note: When creating the plan for deploying a new patch, you should also create a rollback plan.

Note: To ensure that you stay current on new patches, make sure you receive regular security bulletins from Microsoft. To sign up to receive these, go to the Microsoft Security Web site. See the "More Information" section at the end of this chapter for the link.

Categorizing Patches

As each new patch becomes available, you should determine its importance to your environment. This will then determine how soon it will need to be deployed and how much testing you can afford.

Microsoft provides ratings for each vulnerability that is the subject of a security bulletin. The rating levels are shown in the following table.

Table 5.3: Vulnerability Ratings, as Defined by Microsoft

Computer Type	Rating Level		
	Critical	**Moderate**	**Low**
Internet Servers	Web site defacement, denial of service or full control	Difficult to exploit, unusual configuration, or transient effect	Limited impact such as disclosure of scripts
Internal Servers	Elevation of privilege, data disclosure, or modification. Auditing difficult	Auditable data disclosure, modification, or denial of service	Untargeted or fragmentary data theft or modification, limited denial of service
Client Systems	Run arbitrary code without user action; remote escalation of privilege	Local escalation of privilege; untargeted data disclosure or denial of service; exploitation of user actions	Limited or fragmentary data theft or modification; hostile Web site attacks

The rating system categorizes vulnerabilities, according to potential impact if the vulnerability is exploited and likelihood of that happening.

Note: You can use this rating system as a guide for categorizing patches. However, Microsoft's rating system is just an overall estimate of potential impact in the context of millions of customers worldwide; the severity ratings are based on past experience and subjective judgment, so they may not be accurate predictors of impact for your environment. Ultimately, you will need to categorize patches based on your own environment.

Testing the Patches

As with any software, patches may not work perfectly in every environment. Ideally, you should thoroughly test any patches that you are going to install in your environment. However, many security patches need to be installed quickly in order to fix potentially serious problems. In many cases you will find your testing procedure is a compromise between the need to solve a security issue and the need to ensure your patch is stable in your environment.

How much testing is appropriate will depend on how you have categorized the patch. Using the Microsoft categorizations, the following table shows the minimum level of testing you should perform for each patch type.

Table 5.4: Minimum Testing for Patches

Patch Type	Testing Should Consist of
Critical Severity Patches	Assessing the patch Assessing server operations (Limited)
Moderate Severity Patches	Assessing the patch Installing the patch in a test environment Assessing server operations (Full) Checking the uninstall procedure
Low Severity Patches	Assessing the patch Installing the patch in a test environment Assessing server operations (Full) Assessing application operations Checking the uninstall procedure

As part of your risk management procedure you will need to determine how thoroughly you perform each step. If you do skip some of these phases due to urgency, you should still continue to complete them in a test lab in order to try to find potential problems before they occur on already deployed systems.

All testing should occur on servers that resemble the production servers as much as possible.

Assessing the Patch

As a minimum, your patch assessment should consist of the following steps:

- **Identifying patch owner.** For all patches you should have an identified owner who is responsible for the evaluation of the patch.
- **Reviewing all documentation.** Before applying any service pack, hotfix or security patch, all relevant documentation should be read and peer reviewed. The peer review process is critical as it mitigates the risk of a single person missing critical and relevant points when evaluating the update.

- **Verifying the patch category.** It may be that on further assessment of the patch you need to change its category. This will affect other aspects of your testing.

As you read the documentation, look for the following:

- Is the update relevant and will it resolve an outstanding issue?
- Will adopting the update cause other problems resulting in a compromise of the production system?
- Are there dependencies relating to the update? (For example, certain features being enabled or disabled for the update to be effective.)
- Do you need to perform any actions prior to deploying the update?

As well as examining the documentation released with the updates, you should search the Microsoft support Web site for any additional post-release information on the update. TechNet also provides security bulletins in a searchable (by product name and service pack) database on its Web site. These materials supply critical information that must be referenced.

Installing

You should make sure the patch installs as it is supposed to, understand if it requires a reboot, know how much space it takes up (including an uninstall folder), understand what options are available to you, and so on. As well as installing the patch you should read any supporting documentation for additional information.

Server Operations

Once the patch is installed, you need to make sure that the server continues to work normally. It is also a good idea to monitor the Event Log and System Monitor for any unexpected results. Test all the server functions and make sure everything operates as normal. How much risk you can handle on the particular server, for the particular vulnerability, will determine how long you should allow the server to run before determining if everything is running normally. If there are any problems, you will need to make sure these are documented and that you have evaluated the pros and cons of applying the patch. If problems are encountered, they should be reported to Microsoft as soon as possible.

Note: You can use Microsoft Operations Manager to collect Event Log and System Monitor information.

Application Operations

As part of your testing procedure, it is important to test the patch with any applications that coexist on the servers and make sure that you identify any issues with dependencies. After installing the patch you should check that all applications continue to work as before.

Uninstall

It is possible that despite your testing, after installing the patch you will run into problems which result in you needing to uninstall the patch. It is important, therefore, to test that the uninstall works. After uninstalling, you should check that the server continues to run as expected and continue to watch Event Log and System Monitor counters.

Creating a Back Out Plan

Even if your testing proceeds entirely without incident, it is still possible that there will be problems as you deploy the patch throughout your organization. You will therefore need a plan of action to restore the system to its original state before the patch was deployed. In some cases this will consist of taking a snapshot backup of a server before the install occurs, so that if there are problems the server can be restored very quickly. What ever your back out plan, make sure you test it thoroughly.

Deploying the Patches

Assuming your testing proceeds smoothly, you should now be ready to deploy the patch across your organization. There are a number of ways you can do this. These include:

- Manual
- Group Policies
- Scripts

Note: For additional information on deploying patches, see the TechNet article, "Best Practices for Applying Service Packs, Hotfixes and Security Patches." See the "More Information" section at the end of the chapter for the link.

Manual

Manual installation of hotfixes is the most common installation method at most organizations. This consists of simply running the executable corresponding to the hotfix on each server. If your organization has many servers this may be an impractical option.

The name of most hotfixes will tell you important information about the fix. For example, a typical name for a hotfix is Q292435_W2K_SP3_x86_en.EXE. In this case:

- Q292435 is the Knowledge Base article number where you can find out more information about the hotfix.
- W2K is the product it is intended for (Microsoft Windows 2000)
- SP3 is the Service Pack it will be included in.

- x86 is the Processor architecture it is meant for.
- en is the language (English).

Note: Hotfixes that have a file name of QXXXXXX.exe and do not have W2K_SP3_x86 appended to the file name are specific to applications such as Internet Explorer.

Hotfixes also support several command line switches that can be used to control the behavior of the hotfix installation process.

Table 5.5: Switches for Hotfix Executables

Switch	Description
-y	Perform uninstall
-f	Force applications to close at shutdown
-n	Do not create an uninstall directory
-z	Do not reboot when update completes
-q	Quiet mode — no user interface
-m	Unattended mode
-l	List installed hotfixes

Note: Application specific hotfixes with file names of QXXXXXX.exe, typically do not support all of the above switches.

If you script the installation of multiple hotfixes, you will want to use the **-q** and **-z** switches so that the hotfix is installed without a user interface and does not force a reboot.

Normally when you install multiple hotfixes you need to reboot the computer between each one. This is because any files that are locked, or in use, cannot be replaced, so they are placed in a queue to be replaced after the system restarts. QChain is a tool that allows you to string together several hotfixes with only a single reboot, instead of a reboot between each install. To use QChain, run the hotfix installer with the **-z** switch to instruct the installer not to reboot after the installation. Then run QChain.exe and reboot the computer.

Note: QChain is available on TechNet. For further details, see the "More Information" section at the end of this chapter.

If additional components, such as DNS, are added after applying a service pack and patches, it is necessary to reapply the service pack and patches to ensure that the new component is properly patched.

Group Policy

Windows 2000 natively supports software distribution using Group Policy. Patches do not normally come as a Windows Installer package. However, you could use the executable in conjunction with a .zap file.

Applications that do not use Windows Installer packages must use a .zap file to describe their existing setup program. A .zap file is a text file (similar to .ini files) that provides information about how to install a program, the application properties, and the entry points that the application should install.

A .zap file can only be assigned to a user though, which means that once you set up Group Policy to distribute the hotfix you still need to log on to the computer with the user account to which the .zap file was assigned.

Note: For more information on creating a .zap file and for assigning it using Group Policy see the Knowledge Base article Q231747, "How to Publish non-MSI Programs with .zap Files."

Scripts

You may wish to create your own VBScripts or batch files to roll out patches. These could be in the form of logon or startup scripts, which check to see the current patch status and then check updates from a centralized server.

Your scripts can include QChain, to ensure that if more than one hotfix is required, only a single reboot is needed.

Monitoring

After you have installed the patches into your production environment, you need to continue to monitor your servers. Make sure you watch the Event Log, and System Monitor counters for problems. If you see any other errors on the computer for the next couple of weeks, you should test to make sure they are not related to the patch you deployed. Also, if you implemented a patch without thorough lab testing because it was critical, you should continue testing the patch in a lab environment afterwards to make sure nothing was missed.

As well as monitoring existing servers, it is very important that you monitor the environment as a whole to ensure that new servers are not brought onto the network and left without the current patches. There should always be a latest build that new servers will receive, and you should monitor to ensure that this happens.

Reviewing

You can only be sure that any process is working properly if you review it. As you complete the patch management process for individual patches, you should review to ensure that the patch was deployed correctly, and that all procedures worked as they should have. This will help to ensure that the process continues to function as it should. As you review the patch management process, you should continue to analyze for further changes to the environment, which will start the patch management process again.

Client Side Patch Management

This chapter covers the server side process of patch management but you should be aware that many times viruses and other threats to the corporate security gain access through the client side.

Most of the items above relate to client side management also, but there are some differences. Most of the time the differences are not so much in what the patch does but how your corporation deals with the process of determining which patches are needed, testing them, and then deploying.

There are a number of tools that will specifically help you with client side patch management.

Windows Update

If you are running a Windows XP client base, an easy way to check for and apply fixes is to use Windows Update. When you go to the Windows Update Web site the computer is scanned and any patches, both security and nonsecurity related, not installed are listed for download.

In order to run Windows Update, you need to be an administrator of the local machine. This can make the tool impractical for many environments.

Windows Update Corporate Edition

The Windows Update Corporate site provides a comprehensive catalog of updates that can be distributed over a corporate network. It is a one-stop location for Windows Update content and Microsoft Windows Hardware Quality Lab (WHQL) logo device drivers.

Windows Update Corporate Edition allows you to:

- Search for the latest software updates and driver updates by keywords, operating system, update type, component type, language, date posted, and manufacturer to find the ones that are most relevant to your corporation.
- Download updates one at a time as needed, or select multiple updates to download into an assembled package, ready to distribute across your network.
- Use the Download History to review previously downloaded updates and where they reside.
- Use the Read This First file provided for each download to get detailed information on each update before downloading. The Read This First files are included with each download package and contain links to relevant Web sites for more information.

Microsoft Baseline Security Analyzer

This is an application available for download from TechNet that helps you to ensure that your Windows 2000 and Windows XP-based systems are secure and up to date. The Baseline Security Analyzer scans one or more systems and returns a report on items such as: missing security patches, weak passwords, Internet Explorer and Outlook Express security settings, and Office macro protection settings. It will provide information on the security issue at hand, how to fix it, and links to additional information about the issue.

Other Tools

By following the recommendations outlined so far in this chapter, you are well on your way to managing patches effectively within your organization. However there are a number of additional tools that you can use to automate the process of patch management still further.

SMS

If you have Microsoft Systems Management Server (SMS) deployed in your organization, you can use it to help you with many of the phases talked about above.

The Microsoft Security Toolkit contains an SMS import utility that can be used to automate the distribution and installation of recommended IIS security fixes. SMS can help you determine which computers need the security fixes, and then deploy the fixes.

The software deployment features of SMS can be used to roll out patches, in your environment, to all computers that have the SMS client. If you create a software package for the patch, you can force an upgrade to all or any collection of computers in your environment. One of the main advantages is that you can monitor which computers have the patch installed. However you will need an SMS administrator or someone with knowledge of creating SMS packages in most cases to correctly roll these out.

Third-party Tools

A number of third-party tools are available to help with patch management. These offer some features not available currently with Microsoft's free tools, such as the ability to deploy fixes and have the status reported back, create groupings of computers with similar update needs, support other products not covered by the tools described above, and have graphical user interface (GUI) command areas for administrative tasks. You should evaluate these features and determine if they are needed within your environment.

- Polaris Group Hotfix/Service Pack Utility

This tool has an easy to use GUI, supports any Microsoft product, can automate the process of deploying service packs and hotfixes so that all computers run on a corporate standard that you specify.

http://www.polarisgroup.com/solutions

- Shavlik Hfnetchkpro

  This is built on the Hfnetchk technology. It has a GUI and allows you to keep a scan history that the command line version does not.

  http://www.shavlik.com/nshc.htm

- Bindview Security Advisor

  Bindview's tool has a GUI to help simplify the process of checking for noncompliant computers. It also has an update service that lets you know when new patches have been released.

  http://www.bindview.com/Solutions/Security/SecAdvisor_bvCtrlW2k.cfm

- Pedestal Software's Security Expressions

  This tool allows administrators to implement security lock down policies on Windows and UNIX machines. It also has the capability to check for hotfixes and automatically download and install them if needed.

  http://www.pedestalsoftware.com/secexp/index.htm

Summary

The vast majority of breaches in IT security come from the exploitation of systems that are not fully up to date with security patches. Good patch management is essential if you are to minimize the security risks you face. Take patch management seriously and you are likely to dramatically reduce the costs associated with security breaches.

More Information

For more information from Symantec on the fundamentals of security, see:

http://securityresponse.symantec.com/avcenter/security/Content/security.articles /fundamentals.of.info.security.html

Further information on Hfnetchk:

http://support.microsoft.com/default.aspx?scid=kb;EN-US;q303215

To download Hfnetchk:

http://www.microsoft.com/downloads/release.asp?releaseid=31154

mssecure.cab download:

http://download.microsoft.com/download/xml/security/1.0/nt5/en-us/mssecure.cab

For more information on how to create a .zap file for use with Group Policy see:

http://support.microsoft.com/default.aspx?scid=kb;EN-US;Q231747

or

http://msdn.microsoft.com/library/default.asp?url=/library/en-us/dnexnt00/html /ewn0085.asp

Qfecheck.exe information and download:

http://support.microsoft.com/default.aspx?scid=kb;EN-US;Q282784

Hotfix.exe information:

http://support.microsoft.com/default.aspx?scid=kb;EN-US;Q184305

Information on Qchain and to download the executable:

http://support.microsoft.com/default.aspx?scid=kb;EN-US;q296861

Information on the Microsoft Security Rating system:

http://www.microsoft.com/technet/treeview/default.asp?url=/technet/security/policy /rating.asp

To receive regular Microsoft Security Bulletins:

http://www.microsoft.com/technet/treeview/default.asp?url=/technet/security/current.asp

Microsoft Security Toolkit:

http://www.microsoft.com/technet/treeview/default.asp?url=/technet/security/tools /stkintro.asp

Microsoft Operations Framework (MOF):

http://www.microsoft.com/business/services/mcsmof.asp

Best Practices for Applying Service Packs, Hotfixes and Security Patches:

http://www.microsoft.com/technet/treeview/default.asp?url=/technet/security/bestprac /bpsp.asp

References/Links

Microsoft TechNet Security Site:

http://www.microsoft.com/technet/treeview/default.asp?url=/TechNet/itsolutions/security /bestprac/secthret.asp

Microsoft Security Best Practices:

http://www.microsoft.com/technet/treeview/default.asp?url=/TechNet/itsolutions/security /bestprac/secthret.asp

How to Publish non-MSI Programs with .zap Files (Q231747):

http://support.microsoft.com/default.aspx?scid=kb;EN-US;Q231747

6

Auditing and Intrusion Detection

In any secure environment you should actively monitor for intrusion and attack. It would be very foolish to put secure systems in place and then assume you will not be attacked.

There are a number of reasons why auditing and monitoring for intrusion are very important. These include:

- Any functional computer environment is potentially open to attack. No matter how high your security, there is a risk that you may be attacked.
- Successful attacks often follow a series of unsuccessful attacks. If you do not monitor for attacks you will not catch attacks before they are successful.
- If a successful attack does occur, the earlier you find out the easier it will be to contain the damage.
- If you are to recover from attack, you need to know what damage has been done.
- Auditing and intrusion detection helps you determine who was responsible for attack.
- The combination of auditing and intrusion detection helps correlate information to identify attack patterns.
- Regular review of security logs helps identify unknown security configuration issues, such as incorrect permissions, or lax account lockout settings.
- After an attack is detected, auditing can assist in determining what network resources are compromised.

This chapter shows how to audit your environment to give you the best chances of spotting attack, and looks at monitoring for intrusion—including the use of intrusion detection systems—software specifically designed to spot behavior that indicates an attack is occurring.

Auditing

As part of your overall security strategy you should determine the level of auditing appropriate for your environment. Auditing should identify attacks, either successful or not, that pose a threat to your network, or against resources that you determine to be valuable as part of your risk assessment.

When deciding how much to audit, you should bear in mind that the more you audit, the more events you generate, and the more difficult it can be to spot critical events. If you are doing extensive auditing, you should strongly consider using additional tools, such as Microsoft Operations Manager, to help you filter those events which are of greater importance.

Audit events can be split into two categories, success events and failure events. A success event indicates that a user has successfully gained access to a resource, whereas a failure event shows that they tried, but failed. Failure events are very useful in tracking attempted attacks on your environment, but success events are much more difficult to interpret. While the vast majority of successful audit events are simply indications of normal activity, an attacker who manages to gain access to a system will also generate a success event. Often, a pattern of events is as important as the events themselves. For example, a series of failures followed by a success may indicate an attempted attack that was eventually successful.

Wherever possible you should combine audit events with other information you have about your users. For example, if users leave on vacation, you may choose to disable their accounts while they are away, and audit for them being re-enabled.

How to Enable Auditing

Auditing is enabled using Group Policy, at the site, domain, OU or local machine level. You will find the audit policy settings in:

Computer Configuration\Windows Settings\Security Settings\Local Policies\Audit Policy

Generally, you should implement auditing at a high level in the Active Directory hierarchy as this will help to maintain consistency in your auditing settings. In this guide we implement auditing at the Member Server and Domain Controller OU level (see Chapter 4, "Securing Servers Based on Role" for more information).

You may have servers that you have chosen to keep separate from the domain. Auditing can be configured on these machines by editing Group Policy for the local machine, or by using the Auditpol.exe utility in the *Windows 2000 Server Resource Kit*.

Note: To access Group Policy for a local machine, start MMC and then add the Group Policy snap-In, making the Local Computer the focus of the snap-in.

Defining Event Log Settings

Every event generated by auditing will appear in Event Viewer. You should determine how event log will store the events that are generated. Each of the settings can be defined directly in Event Viewer, or in Group Policy. For this guide, we have defined Event Viewer settings in Group Policy. For details of the settings we recommend, see Chapter 4, "Securing Servers Based on Role."

You may wish to modify the settings defined in Group Policy, or apply settings at a different level. For example, you may find your security log is filling up on IIS servers, causing the system to shut down. To prevent this, modify Group Policy at the IIS Server OU to increase the size of the security log, or change the policy so the system does not shut down when the security log is full. To define security log settings in the Group Policy, use the following procedure:

▶ **To modify event log settings using Group Policy on an OU**

1. Click **Start**, select **Administrative Tools**, select **Active Directory Users and Computers**.

2. In the console tree, right-click the OU where you wish to define the audit policy, and then click **Properties**.

3. Select the **Group Policy** tab, select the **Group Policy Object** you wish to edit, and then click **Edit**.

4. In the Group Policy Editor, navigate to **Computer Configuration\Windows Settings\Security Settings\Event Logs\Settings for Event Logs**.

5. Modify the settings according to your requirements.

If you remove the Event Viewer settings from Group Policy, you can instead define them directly in Event Viewer. However, we recommend that you define your Event Viewer settings in Group Policy to ensure consistent settings across similar computers.

Events to Audit

Windows 2000 provides several categories of auditing for security events. When designing your enterprise audit strategy, you will need to decide whether to include the following categories of security audit events:

- Logon events
- Account Logon events
- Object Access
- Directory Service Access
- Privilege Use
- Process tracking
- System events
- Policy change

The following sections detail some of the more common event IDs that are returned when auditing is enabled for specific categories.

Note: Tools used to search and collect event log information are discussed in the "Passive Detection Methods" section later in this chapter.

Logon Events

If you audit for logon events, every time a user logs on or logs off at a computer, an event is generated in the security log of the computer where the logon attempt occurs. Also, when a user connects to a remote server, a logon event is generated in the security log of the remote server. Logon events are created when the logon session and token are created or destroyed, respectively.

Logon events can be useful to track attempts to logon interactively at servers or to investigate attacks launched from a particular computer. Success audits generate an audit entry when a logon attempt succeeds. Failure audits generate an audit entry when a logon attempt fails.

Note: Logon events include both computer and user logon events. You will see separate security event log entries for both the computer account and the user account if a network connection is attempted from a Windows NT – or Windows 2000-based computer. Windows 9x-based computers do not have computer accounts in the directory, and do not generate computer logon event entries for network logon events.

As part of the Member Server and Domain Controller Baseline Policies, auditing for success and failure logon events is enabled. You should therefore expect to see the following event IDs for interactive logons, and Terminal Services logons connecting to computers running Terminal Services.

Table 6.1: Logon Events that Appear in Event Log

Event ID	Description
528	A user successfully logged on to a computer.
529	The logon attempt was made with an unknown user name or a known user name with a bad password.
530	The user account tried to log on outside of the allowed time.
531	A logon attempt was made using a disabled account.
532	A logon attempt was made using an expired account.
533	The user is not allowed to log on at this computer.
534	The user attempted to log on with a logon type that is not allowed, such as network, interactive, batch, service, or remote interactive.
535	The password for the specified account has expired.

Event ID	Description
536	The Net Logon service is not active.
537	The logon attempt failed for other reasons.
538	A user logged off.
539	The account was locked out at the time the logon attempt was made. This event can indicate that a password attack was launched unsuccessfully resulting in the account being locked out.
540	Successful Network Logon. This event indicates that a remote user has successfully connected from the network to a local resource on the server, generating a token for the network user.
682	A user has reconnected to a disconnected Terminal Services session. This event indicates that a previous Terminal Services session was connected to.
683	A user disconnected a Terminal Services session without logging off. This event is generated when a user is connected to a Terminal Services session over the network. It appears on the terminal server.

The following security events can be diagnosed using logon event entries:

- **Local logon attempt failures.** Any of the following Event IDs indicates failed logon attempts: 529, 530, 531, 532, 533, 534, and 537. You will see events 529 and 534 if an attacker tries and fails to guess a username and password combination for a local account. However, these events can also occur when a user forgets their password, or starts browsing the network through My Network Places. In a large scale environment it can be difficult to interpret these events effectively. As a rule, you should investigate these patterns if they occur repeatedly or coincide with other unusual factors. For example, a number of 529 events followed by a 528 event in the middle of the night could indicate a successful password attack (although it could just be an over-tired administrator.)

- **Account misuse.** Events 530, 531, 532, and 533 can all represent misuse of a user account. The events indicate that the account/password combination was correctly entered, but other restrictions are preventing a successful log on. Wherever possible, you should investigate these events to determine if misuse occurred, or if the current restriction needs to be modified. For example, you may need to extend the logon hours of certain accounts.

- **Account lockouts.** Event 539 indicates that an account was locked out. This can indicate that a password attack has failed. You should look for earlier 529 events by the same user account to try and discern the pattern of attempted logons.

- **Terminal Services attacks.** Terminal Services sessions can be left in a connected state that allows processes to continue running after the session is ended. Event ID 683 indicates when a user does not log out from the Terminal Services session, and Event ID 682 indicates when a connection to a previously disconnected session has occurred.

Account Logon Events

When a user logs on to a domain, the log on is processed at a domain controller. If you audit Account Logon events at domain controllers, you will see this logon attempt recorded at the domain controller that validates the account. Account Logon events are created when an authentication package validates a user's credentials. When domain credentials are used, Account Logon events are only generated in domain controllers' event logs. If the credentials presented are local SAM database credentials, then the account logon events are created in the server's security event log.

Because the Account Logon event can be recorded at any valid domain controller in the domain, you must ensure that you consolidate the security log across domain controllers to analyze all Account Logon events in the domain.

Note: As with Logon events, Account Logon events include both computer and user logon events.

As part of the Member Server and Domain Controller Baseline Policies, auditing for success and failure Account Logon events are enabled. You should therefore expect to see the following event IDs for network logons and Terminal Services authentication.

Table 6.2: Account Logon Events that Appear in Event Log

Event ID	Description
672	An authentication service (AS) ticket was successfully issued and validated.
673	A ticket granting service (TGS) ticket was granted.
674	A security principal renewed an AS ticket or TGS ticket.
675	Pre-authentication failed.
676	Authentication Ticket Request Failed
677	A TGS ticket was not granted.
678	An account was successfully mapped to a domain account.
680	Identifies the account used for the successful logon attempt. This event also indicates the authentication package used to authenticate the account.
681	A domain account log on was attempted.
682	A user has reconnected to a disconnected Terminal Services session.
683	A user disconnected a Terminal Services session without logging off.

For each of these events, the event log shows detailed information about each specific log on. The following security events can be diagnosed using account logon event entries:

- **Domain logon attempt failures.** Event IDs 675 and 677 indicate failed attempts to logon to the domain.
- **Time synchronization issues.** If a client computer's time differs from the authenticating domain controller's by more than five minutes (by default), Event ID 675 will appear in the security log.
- **Terminal Services attacks.** Terminal Services sessions can be left in a connected state that allows processes to continue running after the terminal server session is ended. Event ID 683 indicates when a user does not log out from the Terminal Services session, and Event ID 682 indicates when a connection to a previously disconnected session has occurred. To prevent disconnections, or to terminate these disconnected sessions, define the **time interval to end disconnected session** in the Terminal Services Configuration console, in the properties of the RDP-Tcp protocol.

Account Management

Account Management auditing is used to determine when users or groups are created, changed, or deleted. This audit can be used to determine when a security principal was created, and who performed the task.

As part of the Member Server and Domain Controller Baseline Policies, auditing for success and failure in Account Management is enabled. You should therefore expect to see the following event IDs recorded in the security log.

Table 6.3: Account Management Events that Appear in Event Log

Event ID	Description
624	User Account Created
625	User Account Type Change
626	User Account Enabled
627	Password Change Attempted
628	User Account Password Set
629	User Account Disabled
630	User Account Deleted
631	Security Enabled Global Group Created
632	Security Enabled Global Group Member Added
633	Security Enabled Global Group Member Removed

(continued)

Event ID	Description
634	Security Enabled Global Group Deleted
635	Security Disabled Local Group Created
636	Security Enabled Local Group Member Added
637	Security Enabled Local Group Member Removed
638	Security Enabled Local Group Deleted
639	Security Enabled Local Group Changed
641	Security Enabled Global Group Changed
642	User Account Changed
643	Domain Policy Changed
644	User Account Locked Out

The following Account Management events can be diagnosed using security log entries:

- **Creation of a user account.** Event IDs 624 and 626 identify when user accounts are created and enabled. If account creation is limited to specific individuals in the organization, you can use these events to identify whether unauthorized personnel have created user accounts.

- **User account password changed.** The modification of a password by someone other than the user can indicate that an account has been taken over by another user. Look for Event IDs 627 and 628 which indicate that a password change is attempted and is successful. Review the details to determine if a different account performed the change, and whether the account is a member of the help desk or other service team that resets user account passwords.

- **User account status changed.** An attacker may attempt to cover their tracks by disabling or deleting the account used during an attack. All occurrences of Event IDs 629 and 630 should be investigated to ensure that these are authorized transactions. Also look for occurrences of Event ID 626 followed by Event ID 629 a short time later. This can indicate that a disabled account was enabled, used, and then disabled again.

- **Modification of Security Groups.** Membership changes to Domain Admins, Administrators, any of the operator groups, or to custom global, universal, or domain local groups that are delegated administrative functions should be reviewed. For global group membership modifications, look for Event IDs 632 and 633. For domain local group membership modifications, look for Event IDs 636 and 637.

- **Account lockout.** When an account is locked out, two events will be logged at the PDC emulator operations master. A 644 event will indicate that the account name was locked out, and then a 642 event is recorded, indicating that the user account is changed to indicate that the account is now locked out. This event is only logged at the PDC emulator.

Object Access

Auditing can be enabled for all objects in a Windows 2000-based network with a system access control list (SACL). A SACL contains a list of users and groups for which actions on the object are to be audited. Almost any object that a user can manipulate in Windows 2000 has a SACL. This includes files and folders on NTFS drives, printers and registry keys.

A SACL is comprised of access control entries (ACEs). Each ACE contains three pieces of information:

- The security principal to be audited
- The specific access types to be audited, called an access mask
- A flag to indicate whether to audit failed access, successful access, or both

If you want events to appear in the security log, you must first enable **Auditing for Object Access** and then define the SACL for each object you wish to audit.

Audits in Windows 2000 are generated when a handle to an object is opened. Windows 2000 uses a kernel-mode security subsystem that only allows programs to access objects through the kernel. This prevents programs from attempting to bypass the security system. Since the kernel memory space is isolated from user mode programs, a program refers to an object through a data structure called a handle. The following is a typical access attempt:

1. A user instructs a program to access an object (for example, **File/Open**).
2. The program requests a handle from the system, specifying what kind of access (read, write, and so on) is desired.
3. The security subsystem compares the DACL on the requested object to the user's token, looking for entries in the DACL that match either the user or a group the user belongs to and also have the access rights that the program requested.
4. The system compares the SACL on the requested object to the user's token, looking for entries in the SACL that match either the effective rights being returned to the program, or the rights requested by the program. If a matching failure audit ACE matches an access that was requested but not granted, a failure audit event is generated. If a matching success audit ACE matches an access that was granted, a success audit event is generated.
5. If any access is granted, the system returns a handle to the program, which can then use the handle to access the object.

It is very important to note that when auditing occurs and the event is generated, *nothing has happened to the object yet*. This is critical to interpreting audit events. Write audits are generated before a file is written to, and read audits are generated before a file is read.

As with all auditing, it is very important to take a targeted approach to auditing object access. In your auditing plan, decide on the type of objects that you must audit and then determine what type of access attempts (success, failure or both) you wish to monitor for each type of audited object. An overly broad approach to auditing will have a significant impact on your system's performance and will result in the collection of much more data than is necessary or useful.

Generally you will want to audit all access to your chosen objects, including from nontrusted accounts. To achieve this, add the Everyone Group to the SACL on the objects you wish to audit. You should be wary of auditing for success on object access as this can create a very large number of audit entries in the security log. However, if, for example, you are investigating the deletion of a critical file, you will need to examine success audit events to determine which user account deleted the file.

The Member Server and Domain Controller Baseline Policies are set to audit for both success and failure on object access. However, no SACLs are set on the objects themselves and you will need to set these according to the needs of your environment. The SACLs can be defined directly at the objects, or using Group Policy. If the object that requires auditing exists on multiple computers, you should define the SACLs in Group Policy.

Auditing for Object Access will cause the following events to appear in the security log.

Table 6.4: Object Access Events that Appear in Event Log

Event ID	Description
560	Access was granted to an already existing object.
562	A handle to an object was closed.
563	An attempt was made to open an object with the intent to delete it. (This is used by file systems when the FILE_DELETE_ON_CLOSE flag is specified.)
564	A protected object was deleted.
565	Access was granted to an already existing object type.

If you are looking for specific object access events, you will primarily need to research Event ID 560 events. The useful information is within the event details and you will need to search the event details to find the specific events you are searching for. Table 6.5 shows some actions you may need to perform and how to perform them.

Table 6.5: How to Perform Key Auditing Actions for Object Access Event 560

Auditing Action	How it is achieved
Find a specific file, folder or object	In the Event 560 details, search for the full path of the file or folder you wish to review actions for.
Determine actions by a specific user	Define a filter that identifies the specific user in a 560 event.
Determine actions performed at a specific computer	Define a filter that identifies the specific computer account where the task was performed in a 560 event.

Directory Service Access

Active Directory objects have SACLs associated with them and so can be audited. As previously mentioned, you audit Active Directory user and group accounts by auditing Account Management. However, if you want to audit the modification of objects in other naming contexts, such as the Configuration and Schema naming contexts, you must audit for object access, and then define the SACL for the specific containers you wish to audit. Audit entries are generated when users listed on the SACL of an Active Directory object attempt to access that object.

You can modify the SACL for containers and objects in the Configuration naming context (and other naming contexts) using the ADSIEDIT MMC snap-in. This is accomplished by displaying the required context in the ADSIEDIT console, and then modifying the SACL for the object in the **Advanced Security Settings** dialog box.

It is very difficult to find specific events for directory service access, due to the large volume of (generally innocuous) events that take place. For this reason, the Member Server and Domain Controller Baseline Policies only audit failed events for directory service access. This will help you identify when an attacker attempts unauthorized access to Active Directory.

Attempted directory access will show as a directory service event with the ID 565 in the security log. Only by looking at the details of the security event, can you determine which object the event corresponds to.

Privilege Use

As users work in an IT environment, they exercise defined user rights. If you audit Privilege Use for success and failure, an event will be generated each time a user attempts to exercise a user right.

Even if you do audit Privilege Use not all user rights are audited. By default, the following user rights are excluded:

● Bypass traverse checking
● Debug programs
● Create a token object

- Replace process level token
- Generate security audits
- Back up files and directories
- Restore files and directories

You can override the default behavior of not auditing Backup and Restore user rights by enabling the **Audit use of Backup and Restore Privilege** security option in Group Policy.

Auditing for success on Privilege Use will create a very large number of entries in the security log. For this reason, the Member Server and Domain Controller Baseline Policies only audit for failure on Privilege Use.

The following events are generated if auditing for Privilege Use is enabled.

Table 6.6: Privilege Use Events that Appear in Event Log

Event ID	Description
576	Specified privileges were added to a user's access token. (This event is generated when the user logs on.)
577	A user attempted to perform a privileged system service operation.
578	Privileges were used on an already open handle to a protected object.

Here are examples of some of the event log entries that can exist when specific user rights are used:

- **Act as part of the operating system.** Look for Event ID 577 or 578 with SeTcbPrivilege privilege indicated. The user account that made use of the user right is identified in the event details. This event can indicate a user's attempt to elevate security privileges by acting as part of the operating system. For example, the GetAdmin attack, where a user attempted to add their account to the Administrators group used this privilege. The only entries for this event should be for the System account, and any service accounts assigned this user right.

- **Change the system time.** Look for Event ID 577 or 578 with SeSystemtimePrivilege privilege indicated. The user account that used the user right is identified in the event details. This event can indicate a user's attempt to change the system time to hide the true time that an event takes place.

- **Force shutdown from a remote system.** Look for Event IDs 577 and 578 with user right SeRemoteShutdownPrivilege. The specific security identifier (SID) the user right is assigned to and the user name of the security principal that assigned the right are included in the event details.

- **Load and unload device drivers.** Look for Event ID 577 or 578 with SeLoadDriverPrivilege privilege indicated. The user account that made use of this user right is identified in the event details. This event can indicate a user's attempt to load an unauthorized or Trojan horse version of a device driver.

- **Manage auditing and security log.** Look for Event ID 577 or 578 with SeSecurityPrivilege privilege indicated. The user account that made use of this user right is identified in the event details. This event will occur both when the event log is cleared, and when events for privilege use are written to the security log.
- **Shut down the system.** Look for Event ID 577 with SeShutdownPrivilege privilege indicated. The user account that made use of this user right is identified in the event details. This event will occur when an attempt to shut down the computer takes place.
- **Take ownership of files or other objects.** Look for Event ID 577 or 578 with SeTakeOwnershipPrivilege privilege indicated. The user account that used the user right is identified in the event details. This event can indicate that an attacker is attempting to bypass current security settings by taking ownership of an object.

Process Tracking

If you audit detailed tracking information for processes running on Windows 2000-based computers, the event log will show attempts to create processes and end processes. It will also record when a process attempts to generate a handle to an object or obtain indirect access to an object.

Due to the very large number of audit entries created, the Member Server and Domain Controller Baseline Policies do not enable auditing for process tracking. However, if you choose to audit for success and failure the following event IDs will be recorded in the event log.

Table 6.7: Process Tracking Events that Appear in Event Log

Event ID	Description
592	A new process was created.
593	A process exited.
594	A handle to an object was duplicated.
595	Indirect access to an object was obtained.

System Events

System events are generated when a user or process alters aspects of the computer environment. You can audit for attempts to make changes to the system, such as shutting down the computer or altering the system time.

If you audit system events, you also audit when the security log is cleared. This is very important, because attackers will often attempt to clear their tracks after making changes in an environment.

The Member Server and Domain Controller Baseline Policies audit system events for success and failure. This will lead to the following event IDs in the event log.

Table 6.8: System Events that Appear in Event Log

Event ID	Description
512	Windows is starting up.
513	Windows is shutting down.
514	An authentication package was loaded by the Local Security Authority.
515	A trusted logon process has registered with the Local Security Authority.
516	Internal resources allocated for the queuing of security event messages have been exhausted, leading to the loss of some security event messages.
517	The security log was cleared.
518	A notification package was loaded by the Security Accounts Manager.

You can use these event IDs to capture a number of security issues:

- **Computer shutdown/restart.** Event ID 513 shows Windows shutting down. It is important to know when servers have been shut down or rebooted. There are a number of legitimate reasons, such as a driver or application was installed requiring a reboot, or the server was shut down or restarted for maintenance. However, an attacker may also force a reboot of a server in order to gain access to the system during startup. All cases where the computer is shut down should be noted for comparison with the event log.

  Many attacks involve the restart of a computer. By investigating the event logs, you can determine when a server has been restarted, and whether the restart was a planned restart, or an unplanned restart. Event ID 513 shows Windows starting up, as will a series of other events which are automatically generated in the system log. These would include Event ID 6005, which indicates that the Event Log service has started.

  In addition to this entry, look for the existence of one of two different event log entries in the system log. If the previous shutdown was clean, such as when an administrator restarts the computer, then Event ID 6006, the Event Log service was stopped, is recorded in the system log. By examining the details of the entry, you can determine which user initiated the shutdown.

  If the restart was due to an unexpected restart, an Event ID 6008, the previous system shutdown at <*time*> on <*date*> was unexpected. This can be indicative of a denial of service attack that caused a shutdown of the computer. But remember, it also can be due to a power failure, or device driver failure as well.

If the restart was due to a blue screen, an Event ID 1001, with a source of Save Dump, is recorded in the system log. The actual blue screen error message can be reviewed in the event details.

Note: To include the recording of Event ID 1001 entries, the option to **Write an event to the system log** check box must be enabled in the recovery settings section of the System Control Panel applet.

- **Modifying or Clearing of the Security Log.** An attacker may try to modify the security logs, or disable auditing during an attack, or clear the security log to prevent detection. If you notice large blocks of time with no entries in the security log, you should look for Event IDs 612 and 517 to determine which user modified the audit policy. All occurrences of Event ID 517 should be compared to a physical log indicating all times that the security log was cleared. An unauthorized clearing of the security log can be an attempt to hide events that existed in the previous security log. The name of the user that cleared the log is included in the event details.

Policy Change

Your audit policy defines which changes to your environment are audited, helping you to determine if there have been attempts to attack your environment. However, a determined attacker will look to alter the audit policy itself, so that any changes they make are not audited.

If you audit for policy change, you will show attempts to alter the audit policy, alongside changes to other policies and user rights. The Member Server and Domain Controller Baseline Policies audit policy change for success and failure. You will see these events recorded in the event log.

Table 6.9: Policy Change Events that Appear in Event Log

Event ID	Description
608	A user right was assigned.
609	A user right was removed.
610	A trust relationship with another domain was created.
611	A trust relationship with another domain was removed.
612	An audit policy was changed.
768	A collision was detected between a namespace element in one forest and a namespace element in another forest (occurs when a namespace element in one forest overlaps a namespace element in another forest).

The two most important events to look for here are Event IDs 608 and 609. A number of attempted attacks may result in these events being recorded. The following examples will all generate Event ID 608 if the user right is assigned or 609 if it is removed. In each case the specific SID that the user right is assigned to, along with the user name of the security principal that assigned the right is included in the event details:

- **Act as part of the operating system.** Look for Event IDs 608 and 609 with user right seTcbPrivilege in the event details.

- **Add workstations to the domain.** Look for the events with user right SeMachineAccountPrivilege in the event details.

- **Back up files and directories.** Look for the events with user right SeBackupPrivilege in the event details.

- **Bypass traverse checking.** Look for events with user right SeChangeNotifyPrivilege in the event details. This user right allows users to traverse a directory tree even if the user has no other permissions to access that directory.

- **Change the system time.** Look for events with user right SeSystemtimePrivilege in the event details. This user right allows a security principal to change the system time, potentially masking when an event takes place.

- **Create permanent shared objects.** Look for events with user right SeCreatePermanentPrivilege in the event details. The holder of this user right can create file and print shares.

- **Debug programs.** Look for events with user right SeDebugPrivilege in the event details. A holder of this user right can attach to any process. This right is, by default, only assigned to Administrators.

- **Force shutdown from a remote system.** Look for events with user right SeRemoteShutdownPrivilege in the event details.

- **Increase scheduling priority.** Look for events with user right SeIncreaseBasePriorityPrivilege in the event details. A user with this right can modify process priorities.

- **Load and unload device drivers.** Look for events with user right SeLoadDriverPrivilege in the event details. A user with this user right could load a Trojan horse version of a device driver.

- **Manage auditing and security log.** Look for events with user right SeSecurityPrivilege in the event details. A user with this user right can view and clear the security log.

- **Replace a process level token.** Look for events with user right SeAssignPrimaryTokenPrivilege in the event details. A user with this user right can change the default token associated with a started subprocess.

- **Restore files and directories.** Look for events with user right SeRestorePrivilege in the event details.
- **Shut down the system.** Look for events with user right SeShutdownPrivilege in the event details. A user with this user right could shut down the system to initialize the installation of a new device driver.
- **Take ownership of files or other objects.** Look for events with user right SeTakeOwnershipPrivilege in the event details. A user with this user right can access any object or file on an NTFS disk by taking ownership of the object or file.

Note: These audit events only identify that the user right was assigned to a specific security principal. It does not mean that the security principal has performed a task using the user right. The audit events do determine when the user right policy was modified.

Note: For more information on use of user rights, see *"Writing Secure Code"* by Michael Howard and David LeBlanc (Microsoft Press, ISBN: 0-7356-1588-8).

Protecting Event Logs

To ensure that the event log entries are maintained for future reference, you should take a number of steps to protect the security of the event logs. These should include:

- Defining a policy for the storage, overwriting and maintenance of all event logs. The policy should define all required event log settings and be enforced by Group Policy.
- Ensure that the policy includes how to deal with full event logs, especially the security log. It is recommended that a full security log require the shutdown of the server. This may not be practical for some environments, but you should certainly consider it
- Prevent guest access to the event logs by enabling the security policy settings to prevent local guests from accessing the system, application, and security logs.
- Ensure that the system events are audited for both success and failure to determine if any attempts are made to erase the contents of the security log.
- All security principals that have the ability to view or modify audit settings, must use complex passwords or two factor authentication methods such as smart card logon, to prevent attacks against these accounts to gain access to audit information.

These settings are all defined in the Member Server and Domain Controller Group Policy Objects shown in Chapter 4, "Securing Servers Based on Role."

In addition to these steps, you should take some further practical measures to ensure that your event log information is as safe as possible:

- Your security plan should also include physical security of all servers to ensure that an attacker cannot gain physical access to the computer where auditing is performed. An attacker can remove audit entries by modifying or deleting the physical *.evt files on the local disk subsystem.

- Implement a method to remove or store the event logs in a location separate from the physical server. These can include using Scheduled Tasks to write the event logs to CDR or write once, read many media at regular intervals, or to other network locations separate from the server. If the backups are copied to external media such as backup tapes, or CDR media, the media should be removed from the premises in the event of fire or other natural disasters.

Note: Preventing guest access to event logs only restricts nondomain members from accessing the event logs. By default, all users in a domain can access the system and application logs. Only access to the security log is restricted. Security principals that are assigned the user right **Manage auditing and security log** can access the security log. By default, this is only assigned to Administrators and Exchange Enterprise Servers.

Other Auditing Best Practices

In addition to configuring auditing, there are other practices that should be implemented to effectively audit the security of your server environment. These include:

- Scheduling regular review of the event logs
- Reviewing other application log files
- Monitoring installed services and drivers
- Monitoring open ports

Scheduling Regular Review of the Event Logs

As mentioned previously, the security log and potentially the other event logs should be written to either removable material or consolidated to a central location for review. The review of the logs is the most often missed step of auditing.

You must ensure that a single person or a team has the review of the event logs as a regular task in their job description. The review of event logs can be scheduled as a daily or weekly event, depending on the amount of data that is collected in the security log. This is typically based on the level of auditing implemented on the network. If more events are included in the audit, the volume of log entries will be larger. If you schedule regular event log reviews you will help achieve the following:

- **Faster detection of security issues.** If daily review of the event logs is performed, a security event should never be older than 24 hours old. This leads to faster detection, and repair, of security vulnerabilities.

- **Define responsibility.** If regular review of event logs is required, the person tasked with reviewing the log files can be ultimately responsible for identifying potential attacks.

- **Reduces the risk of events being overwritten or server down.** Once an event log is reviewed, the events in the log file can be archived for future review, and removed from the current event log. This reduces the risk of the event logs becoming full.

Reviewing other Application Log Files

In addition to reviewing the Windows 2000 event logs for security events, you should also review the logs created by applications. These application logs may include valuable information regarding potential attacks that can supplement the information found in the event logs. Depending on your environment, you may need to look at one or more of these log files:

- **Internet Information Services (IIS).** IIS creates log files that track connection attempts to Web, FTP, network time protocol (NTP), and SMTP services. Each service running under IIS maintains separate log files, and stores the log files in the W3C Extended Log File Format in the %WinDir%\System32\Logfiles folder. Each service maintains a separate folder to further break down the logging information. Alternatively, you can configure IIS to store the logs into an ODBC–compliant database, such as Microsoft SQL Server.

- **Internet Security and Acceleration (ISA) Server.** ISA Server provides logs for packet filters, the ISA Server Firewall Service and the ISA Server Web Proxy Service. As with IIS, the logs are stored in the W3C Extended Log File Format by default, but can be recorded to an ODBC-compliant database as an alternative. The ISA Server log files are stored in the C:\Program Files\Microsoft ISA Server\ISALogs folder by default.

- **Internet Authentication Service (IAS).** IAS provides centralized authentication and accounting for remote access authentication using the Remote Authentication Dial-In User Service (RADIUS) protocol. By default, accounting requests, authentication requests, and periodic status requests are logged to the IASlog.log file located in the %WinDir%\System32\Logfiles folder. Alternatively, the log file can be saved in a database compatible file format, rather than in IAS format.

- **Third-party applications.** Several third-party applications implement local logging functions to provide detailed information on the application. For more information, see the specific help files for your application.

Note: All computers that maintain log files should use synchronized clocks. This allows an administrator to compare events between computers and services to establish what actions were taken by an attacker. For more details on time synchronization, see "The Importance of Time Synchronization" section later in this chapter.

Monitoring Installed Services and Drivers

Many attacks against a computer are implemented by attacking services installed on the target computer, or by replacing valid drivers with versions of the driver that include a Trojan horse, allowing an attacker access to the target computer.

The following tools can be used to monitor the installed services and drivers on your computers:

- **The Services Console.** The Services MMC console is used to monitor the services of either the local computer or a remote computer and allows an administrator to configure, pause, stop, start, and restart all installed services. Use this console to determine if any services configured to start automatically are not currently started.

- **Netsvc.exe.** This command line tool, included in the *Windows 2000 Server Resource Kit*, allows an administrator to remotely start, stop, pause, continue, and query the status of services from the command line.

- **SvcMon.exe.** This tool monitors services on local and remote computers for changes in state (starting or stopping). To detect these changes, Service Monitoring Tool implements a polling system. When a monitored service stops or starts, Service Monitoring Tool notifies you by sending e-mail. You must configure the servers, polling intervals, and services to monitor by using the Service Monitor Configuration Tool (smconfig.exe).

- **Drivers.exe.** This tool displays all installed device drivers at the computer where the tool is executed. The output of the tool includes information that includes the driver's file name, the size of the driver on disk, and the date that the driver was linked. The link date can be used to identify any newly installed drivers. If an updated driver was not recently installed, this can indicate a replaced driver. Always correlate this information with a system restart event in the Event Viewer.

Note: Not all services (such as the Workstation service) can be stopped directly, although you can query them. If the user has a lot of active connections, you cannot force the service to shut down remotely, although you can pause or query it. Some services have other services that are dependent on them; trying to shut down such services will fail unless the dependent services are shut down first.

Monitoring Open Ports

Attacks are often started by performing a port scan to identify any known services running on the target computer. You should make sure that you carefully monitor which ports are open on your servers, which generally means scanning the ports yourself to determine what can be accessed.

When performing port scans, you should perform them both locally at the target computer, and from a remote computer. If the computer can be accessed from a public network, the port scan should be performed from an external computer, to ensure that your firewall software only allows access to desired ports.

Netstat.exe is a command line utility that can show all open ports for both TCP and UDP. The Netstat command uses the following syntax:

```
NETSTAT [-a] [-e] [-n] [-s] [-p proto] [-r] [interval]
```

Where:

- **-a.** Displays all connections and listening ports.
- **-e.** Displays Ethernet statistics. This may be combined with the **-s** option.
- **-n.** Displays addresses and port numbers in numerical form.
- **-p** *proto.* Shows connections for the protocol specified by proto; proto may be TCP or UDP. If used with the **-s** option to display per protocol statistics, proto may be TCP, UDP, or IP.
- **-r.** Displays the routing table.
- **-s.** Displays per protocol statistics. By default, statistics are shown for TCP, UDP and IP; the **-p** option may be used to specify a subset of the default.
- **interval.** Redisplays selected statistics, pausing interval seconds between each display. Press CTRL+C to stop redisplaying statistics. If omitted, netstat will print the current configuration information once.

When you list the open TCP and UDP ports at the local computer, port numbers are translated to names based on the entries in the services file found in the \%WinDir%\System32\Drivers\Etc\ folder. If you prefer to only see port numbers, you can use the **-n** switch.

If any open ports are discovered that are not recognized, you should investigate them to determine if the corresponding service is needed on the computer. If it is not, you should disable or remove the associated service to prevent the computer from listening on that port. A number of services have been disabled in the Member Server and Domain Controller Baseline Policies included with this guide.

Because many servers are protected by firewalls, or packet filtering routers, it is also recommended to perform the port scan from a remote computer. Many third-party tools (including some freeware) are available that can do remote port scans. The remote port scan reveals which ports are available to external users when they attempt to connect to the computer.

Note: Port scanning can also be used to test your intrusion detection system to ensure that it detects the port scan as it is taking place. For more information on intrusion detections systems, see the "Active Detection Methods" section later in this chapter.

Monitoring for Intrusion and Security Events

Monitoring for intrusion and security events includes both passive and active tasks. Many intrusions are detected after the attack has taken place through the inspection of log files. This post-attack detection is often referred to as *passive* intrusion detection. Only through inspection of the log files, can the attack be reviewed and reconstructed based on the log information.

Other intrusion attempts can be detected as the attack takes place. This methodology, known as *active* intrusion detection, looks for known attack patterns, or commands, and blocks the execution of those commands.

This section will look at tools that can be used to implement both forms of intrusion detection to protect your network from attacks.

The Importance of Time Synchronization

When monitoring for both intrusion and security events between multiple computers, it is essential that the computers' clocks are synchronized. Synchronized time allows an administrator to reconstruct what took place during an attack against multiple computers. Without synchronized time, it is very difficult to determine exactly when specific events took place, and how events interlace. More detailed information on time synchronization can be found in Chapter 3, "Managing Security with Windows 2000 Group Policy."

Passive Detection Methods

Passive intrusion detection systems involve the manual review of event logs and application logs. The inspection involves analysis and detection of attack patterns in event log data. There are several tools, utilities, and applications that can help review event logs. This section outlines how each tool can be used to coordinate information.

Event Viewer

The Windows 2000 security log can of course be viewed using the Windows 2000 Event Viewer MMC console. Event Viewer allows you to view the application, security, and system logs. You can define filters to find specific events in the Event Viewer.

▶ **To define filters in the Event Viewer**

1. Select the specific event log in the console tree.

2. Select **Filter** from the view menu.

3. Select the parameters for filtering.

In the **Filter** tab of the **Properties** dialog box, you can define the following attributes to filter event entries:

- **Event types.** The filter can be limited to information, warning, error, success audits, failure audits, or any combination of the event types.
- **Event source.** The specific service or driver that generated the event.
- **Category.** The filter can be limited to specific categories of events.
- **Event ID.** If you know the specific Event ID that you are searching for, the filter can limit the listing to that specific Event ID.
- **User.** You can limit the event display to events generated by a specific user.
- **Computer.** You can limit the event display to events generated by a specific computer
- **Date intervals.** You can limit the display to events that fall between specific beginning and ending dates.

When the filter is applied, the filtered event list can be exported to either a comma separated or tab separated listing for import into a database application.

Dump Event Log Tool (Dumpel.exe)

Dump Event Log is a command-line tool, included in the *Windows 2000 Server Resource Kit, Supplement One* (Microsoft Press, ISBN: 0-7356-1279-X). It will dump an event log for a local or remote system into a tab separated text file. This file could then be imported into a spreadsheet or database for further investigation. The tool can also be used to filter for or filter out certain event types.

The following syntax is used by the dumpel.exe tool:

```
dumpel -f file [-s \\server] [-l log [-m source]] [-e n1 n2 n3...] [-r] [-t] [-d x]
```

Where:

- **-f** *file*. Specifies the file name for the output file. There is no default for **-f**, so you must specify the file.

- **-s** *server*. Specifies the server for which you want to dump the event log. Leading backslashes on the server name are optional.

- **-l** *log*. Specifies which log (system, application, security) to dump. If an invalid logname is specified, the application log is dumped.

- **-m** *source*. Specifies in which source (such as redirector (rdr), serial, and so on) to dump records. Only one source can be supplied. If this switch is not used, all events are dumped. If a source is used that is not registered in the registry, the application log is searched for records of this type.

- **-e** *n1 n2 n3*. Filters for event id *nn* (up to ten can be specified). If the **-r** switch is not used, only records of these types are dumped; if **-r** is used, all records except records of these types are dumped. If this switch is not used, all events from the specified *sourcename* are selected. You cannot use this switch without the **-m** switch.

- **-r**. Specifies whether to filter for specific sources or records, or to filter them out.

- **-t**. Specifies that individual strings are separated by tabs. If **-t** is not used, strings are separated by spaces.

- **-d** *x*. Dumps events for the past *x* days.

Note: Dumpel can only retrieve content from the system, application, and security log files. You cannot use Dumpel to query content from the File Replication Service, DNS, or Directory Service event logs.

EventCombMT

EventCombMT is a multi-threaded tool that will parse event logs from many servers at the same time, spawning a separate thread of execution for each server that is included in the search criteria. The tool allows you to:

- **Define either a single Event ID, or multiple Event IDs to search for.** You can include a single event ID, or multiple event IDs separated by spaces.

- **Define a range of Event IDs to search for.** The endpoints are inclusive. For example, if you want to search for all events between and including Event ID 528 and Event ID 540, you would define the range as 528 > ID < 540. This feature is useful because most applications that write to the event log use a sequential range of events.

- **Limit the search to specific event logs.** You can choose to search the system, application, and security logs. If executed locally at a domain controller, you can also choose to search FRS, DNS and AD logs.

- **Limit the search to specific event message types.** You can choose to limit the search to error, informational, warning, success audit, failure audit, or success events.

- **Limit the search to specific event sources.** You can choose to limit the search to events from a specific event source.

- **Search for specific text within an event description.** With each event, you can search for specific text. This is useful if you are trying to track specific users or groups.

Note: You cannot include search logic, such as AND, OR, or NOT in the specific text. In addition, do not delimit text with quotes.

- **Define specific time intervals to scan back from the current date and time.** This allows you to limit your search to events in the past week, day or month.

Installing the Tool

To install the tool, extract the contents of the self extracting SecurityOps.exe file included with this guide. This will create a C:\SecurityOps\EventComb folder. Once the files are extracted, you can run the EventCombMT tool by double-clicking the EventCombMT.exe file.

Running the EventComb tool

The first step in using the EventComb tool is defining which computers will be included in the event log search.

▶ To add computers to the search

1. In the EventCombMT utility, ensure that the correct domain is autodetected in the domain box. If you wish to search event logs in a different domain, then manually type the new domain name in the **Domain** box.

2. To add computers to the search list, right-click the box below **Select To Search/ Right Click to Add**. The pop-up menu shown in Figure 6.1 is shown:

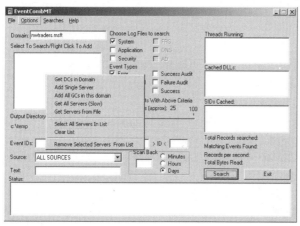

Figure 6.1
Adding computers that were not autodetected to the search list

The following options are available:

- **Get DCs in Domain.** Adds all domain controllers for the current domain to the listing.
- **Add Single Server.** Allows you to add a server or workstation by name to the listing.
- **Add all GCs in this domain.** Allows you to add all domain controllers in the selected domain that are configured to be global catalog servers.
- **Get All Servers.** Adds all servers found in the domain using the browser service. The servers exclude all domain controllers.
- **Get Servers from File.** Allows you to import a file that lists all servers to be included in the search scope. Each server should be entered on a separate line in the text file.

3. Once the servers are added to the list, you must select which servers to perform the search against. When selected, the server will appear highlighted in the list. You can choose multiple servers, using a CTRL+click combination.

Specifying the Event Logs and Event Types to Search

Once you have selected the servers to be included in your event log search, you can narrow the scope of the search by selecting which event logs and event types to include.

In the EventCombMT utility, you can select from the following event logs for the search:

- System
- Application
- Security
- FRS (File Replication Service Log)
- DNS (DNS Server log)
- AD (Directory Service log)

You can also select the Event types to include in the search:

- **Error.** Recorded in the application and system logs, and also appear in the FRS, DNS, and Directory Services logs.
- **Informational.** Recorded in the application and system logs, and also appear in the FRS, DNS, and Directory Services logs.
- **Warning.** Recorded in the application and system logs, and also appear in the FRS, DNS, and Directory Services logs.
- **Success Audit.** Occur in the security log or in the application log if the application registers success audits to the application log. For example, Active Directory Migration Tool (ADMT) logs success audit events to the application log.

- **Failure Audit.** Occur in the security log or in the application log if the application registers failure audits to the application log. For example, ADMT logs failure audit events to the application log

- **Success.** Are very rare and are found in the application or system logs, and also appear in the FRS, DNS, and Directory Services logs. In event viewer, success events are displayed as informational event type.

Note: If you are aware of the specifics of which event log an event ID appears in, and the event type of the event ID, always include this information in your search criteria as it reduces the time for the search.

Saving Searches

EventCombMT allows you to save searches and reload them later. This can be useful if you frequently use EventCombMT to search your IIS servers for one set of events and your domain controllers for another.

Search Criteria are saved in the registry under:
HKLM\Software\Microsoft\EventCombMT and are easily edited.

Search Result Files

The results of the search are saved to the C:\Temp folder by default. The results include a summary file named EventCombMT.txt and for each computer included in the event log search, a separate text file named *ComputerName-EventLogName*_LOG.txt is generated. These individual text files contain all the events extracted from the event logs that match your search criteria.

Examples of Using EventCombMT

To show how EventCombMT can be used, we will show how the tool can be configured to detect domain controller reboots and account lockouts.

▶ **To use EventCombMT to search for restarts of domain controllers**

1. In the EventCombMT tool, ensure that the domain is configured to the correct domain name.

2. In the **Select to Search/Right Click to Add** box below the domain name, right click the box, and then click **Get DCs in Domain**.

Note: When searching for events such as Account Logon and Account Management events, ensure that you search all domain controllers. Because Windows 2000 uses a multi-master model for account management, an account can be added, modified, or deleted at any domain controller in the domain. Likewise, authentication can be validated by any domain controller in the domain. Because of this, you cannot be sure where the specific update or authentication attempt takes place.

3. Right-click the **Select to Search/Right Click to Add** box, and then click **Select All Servers in List**.

4. In the **Choose Log Files to search** section of the tool, select the **System** log only.

5. In the **Event Types** section of the tool, select **Error** and **Informational**.

6. In the **Event IDs** box, type the following Event IDs: **1001 6005 6006 6008**

7. Before clicking the **Search** button, ensure that your search criteria is defined as shown in the figure below, and then click Search.

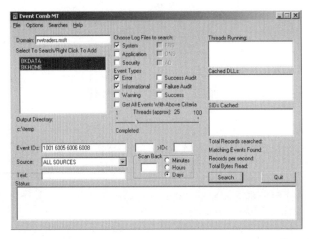

When the search is completed, the results can be viewed in the log directory, which should open automatically when the search is complete.

▶ **To review the log entries**

1. From the **File** menu, select **Open Log Directory**.

2. In the C:\Temp folder, double-click the output file for a domain controller to view the specific events logged by the EventCombMT tool. You should see output similar to the following:

```
1001,INFORMATIONAL,Save Dump,Wed Nov 28 05:45:50 2001,,The computer has
rebooted from a bugcheck.  The bugcheck was:  0x000000d1 (0x00000004,
0x00000002, 0x00000000, 0x84c983dc).  A dump was saved in:
C:\WINDOWS\MEMORY.DMP.
6005,INFORMATIONAL,EventLog,Wed Nov 28 05:45:46 2001,,The Event log service was
started.
6008,ERROR,EventLog,Wed Nov 28 05:45:46 2001,,The previous system shutdown at
5:33:47 AM on 11/28/2001 was unexpected.
6005,INFORMATIONAL,EventLog,Tue Nov 27 14:10:53 2001,,The Event log service was
started.
6006,INFORMATIONAL,EventLog,Tue Nov 27 14:09:26 2001,,The Event log service was
stopped.
6005,INFORMATIONAL,EventLog,Tue Nov 27 10:11:37 2001,,The Event log service was
started.
```

The 6006 events indicate a planned shutdown initiated by a user with the user rights to shutdown the domain controller. The 6005 events indicate that the event log service was started. This occurs at start up time.

The 6008 and 1001 events indicate that the computer was either powered off without shutting down, or restarted because it locked up, or experienced a blue screen. If a 1001 event exists, a blue screen did occur, and the associated debug information and reference to the debug file is included.

The events returned by the EventCombMT tool should be cross-checked with known down time, and nonmatching events should be researched to ensure that the server has not been attacked.

EventCombMT includes several preconfigured searches that can be used to search for security events. For example, there is a predefined search that searches for Account Lockout events.

▶ **To use EventCombMT to search for Account Lockouts**

1. In the EventCombMT tool, ensure that the domain is configured to the correct domain name.

2. In the **Select to Search/Right Click to Add** box below the domain name, right click the box, and then click **Get DCs in Domain**.

3. Right-click the **Select to Search/Right Click to Add** box, and then click **Select All Servers in List**.

4. From the **Searches** menu, click **Built In Searches**, and then click **Account Lockouts**. The EventCombMT utility is configured as shown in the following figure:

5. Click **Search**.

6. When the search is completed, the results can be viewed in the log directory, which should open automatically when the search is complete.

Note: Other predefined searches that are included with EventcombMT include File Replication Services searches, Active Directory searches for duplicate SIDs and NETLOGON DNS registration failures, Hardware disk errors, and DNS interface errors. You can also define and save your own custom searches.

Event Collection

One of the main goals of auditing is to identify the actions taken by attackers on your network. An attacker may attempt to compromise multiple computers and devices on the network, so to understand the extent of any attack, you must be able to coordinate and consolidate information from many computers.

If your log utilities will import into a database, it is easier to coordinate the information from multiple logs. As long as your time is synchronized across all computers, you can sort on time fields, and ease the tracking of events based on time intervals.

The following sections outline some of the tools and utilities that you can use to collect event log information into a central location.

Scripting

Scripts can be written that collect event log information from remote computers and store the information in a central location. By using scripting, you can choose when to run the scripts using Scheduled Tasks and what actions to take once the event log is successfully copied to the central location.

A simple example would be to create a batch file that uses Dumpel.exe from the *Windows 2000 Server Resource Kit,* and launch the batch file at regular intervals using Scheduled Tasks in the Control Panel.

The *Windows 2000 Resource Kit, Supplement One* includes Eventquery.pl. This is a Perl script that displays events from the Event Viewer logs on local and remote computers running Windows 2000 and offers a wide range of filters to help you find specific events.

Note: To use this script, you will need to install ActivePerl from the *Windows 2000 Server Resource Kit.*

Microsoft Operations Manager

Microsoft Operations Manager 2000 offers a comprehensive set of tools that allow enterprises to thoroughly analyze the built-in event reporting and performance monitoring of Windows 2000 and its applications. Operations Manager can collect, store, and report events and performance data to a single location through the use of Intelligent Agents at remote computers, allowing an administrator to centrally review the collected information.

The core Operations Manager management pack collects events that appear in the system, application and security event logs and aggregates the results into a central event repository.

Note: Operations Manager stores its information in a SQL database, and offers several methods to retrieve and analyze the archived data. Administrators can use the Operations Manager Administrator Console, Web Console, or Operations Manager Reporting to view, print, or publish the data. Each view includes predefined views for analyzing the archived data, and allows for customized views and reports to be defined.

Third-party Solutions for Event Log Collection

Several third party products are available which offer centralized collection and inspection of event logs. As you evaluate third-party products, include the following features in your criteria:

- **Support for all Windows 2000 logs.** Support for the DNS Server, Directory Service, and File Replication Service logs in addition to the application, security, and system logs should be provided.
- **Use of a Database Backend.** The tool should allow the event logs to be stored in a database structure that allows inspection of previous event log entries for trend analysis and correlation of events between multiple servers.
- **Search and Reporting Functionality.** The tool should allow you to search for specific events based on provided criteria. The results should be presented in a readable manner.

Third-party products that provide event collection ability include:

- **Event Log Monitor**–TNT Software (www.tntsoftware.com)
- **Event Archiver**–Dorian Software Creations (www.doriansoft.com)
- **LogCaster**–RippleTech (www.rippletech.com)

Active Detection Methods

Active intrusion detection systems analyze incoming network traffic at the application layer, looking for well known attack methods or suspicious application layer payloads. If a suspicious packet is received, the intrusion detection system will typically drop the packet, and log an entry into a log file. Some intrusion detection systems can also alert an administrator if a severe attack is detected.

Inspecting HTTP Access Using URLScan

If you host websites in your organization, some of your servers will receive incoming HTTP traffic. However, not all of this traffic is necessarily legitimate. UrlScan is an ISAPI filter that analyzes incoming HTTP packets and can reject any suspicious traffic.

UrlScan protects a server from attacks by filtering and rejecting HTTP requests for selected IIS service features. By default, UrlScan is configured to accept requests for only static HTML files—including graphics. It will reject the following types of requests:

- CGI (.exe) pages
- WebDAV
- FrontPage Server Extensions
- Index Server
- Internet printing
- Server side includes

UrlScan can be implemented as an end point intrusion detection system by installing the ISAPI filter at all IIS servers on the network or as a network intrusion detection system by installing the UrlScan ISAPI filter on an ISA Server located at the perimeter of your network. If you are using ISA Server as a firewall, you should consider a combination of both solutions. At the network perimeter, block all general unwanted traffic from entering the network. At the end point IIS servers, specific rule sets can be implemented based on the format of the content provided at the Web server.

UrlScan is configured using a file called UrlScan.ini, located in the %WinDir%\system32\inetsrv\Urlscan folder. This file has several sections.

The [Options] section defines how the IIS server will handle both valid and invalid Web requests. The options that can be defined include:

- **UseAllowVerbs.** Allowed values are 0 or 1. If set to the default value of 1, UrlScan reads the AllowVerbs section of UrlScan.ini and rejects any request containing an HTTP verb that is not explicitly listed. The AllowVerbs section is case sensitive. If set to 0, UrlScan reads the DenyVerbs section of UrlScan.ini and rejects any request containing an HTTP verb listed. The DenyVerbs section is not case sensitive.

- **UseAllowExtensions.** Allowed values are 0 or 1. If set to 1, UrlScan reads the AllowExtensions section of UrlScan.ini and rejects any request in which the file extension associated with the URL is not explicitly listed. If set to the default value of 0, UrlScan reads the DenyExtensions section of UrlScan.ini and rejects any request in which the file extension associated with the request is listed. Both the AllowExtensions and DenyExtensions sections are case insensitive.

- **NormalizeUrlBeforeScan.** Allowed values are 0 or 1. If set to the default value of 1, UrlScan does all of its analysis on the request URLs after IIS decodes and normalizes them. If set to 0, UrlScan does all of its analysis on the raw URLs as sent by the client. Only advanced administrators who are very knowledgeable about URL parsing should set this option to 0, as doing so will likely expose the IIS server to canonicalization attacks that bypass proper analysis of the URL extensions.

- **VerifyNormalization.** Allowed values are 0 or 1. If set to the default value of 1, UrlScan verifies normalization of the URL. This action will defend against canonicalization attacks, where a URL contains a double encoded string in the URL (as an example, the string "%252e" is a double encoded '.' character because "%25" decodes to a '%' character, the first pass decoding of "%252e" results in "%2e", which can be decoded a second time into '.'). If set to 0, this verification is not done.

- **AllowHighBitCharacters.** Allowed values are 0 or 1. If set to 1, UrlScan allows any byte to exist in the URL. If set to the default value of 0, UrlScan rejects any request where the URL contains a character outside of the ASCII character set.

This feature can defend against Unicode or UTF-8 based attacks, but will also reject legitimate requests on IIS servers that use a non-ASCII code page.

- **AllowDotInPath.** Allowed values are 0 or 1. If set to the default value of 0, UrlScan rejects any requests containing multiple instances of the dot (.) character. If set to 1, UrlScan does not perform this test. Because UrlScan operates at a level where IIS has not yet parsed the URL, it is not possible to determine in all cases whether a dot character denotes the extension or whether it is a part of the directory path or filename of the URL. For the purposes of extension analysis, UrlScan will always assume that an extension is the part of the URL beginning after the last dot in the string and ending at the first question mark or slash character after the dot or the end of the string. Setting AllowDotInPath to 0 defends against the case where an attacker uses path info to hide the true extension of the request (for example, "/path/TrueURL.asp/BogusPart.htm").

Note: Setting AllowDotInPath to 0 also causes UrlScan to deny any request that contains a dot in a directory name.

- **RemoveServerHeader.** Allowed values are 0 or 1. If set to 1, UrlScan removes the server header on all responses. If set to the default value 0, UrlScan does not perform this action. Note that this feature is only available if UrlScan is installed on IIS 4.0 or later.

- **EnableLogging.** Allowed values are 0 or 1. If set to the default value of 1, UrlScan logs its actions into a file called UrlScan.log, which will be created in the same directory that contains UrlScan.dll. If set to 0, no logging will be done.

- **PerProcessLogging.** Allowed values are 0 or 1. If set to 1, UrlScan appends the process ID of the IIS process hosting UrlScan.dll to the log file name (for example, UrlScan.1234.log). This feature is helpful for IIS versions that can host filters in more than 1 process concurrently. If set to the default value of 0, the log file will be UrlScan.log.

- **AlternateServerName.** Allowed value is a string where the default is an empty string. If this setting is present (the string is not empty) and if RemoveServerHeader is set to 0, IIS replaces its default header in all responses with this string. If RemoveServerHeader is set to 1, AlternateServerName has no meaning. This feature is only available if UrlScan is installed on IIS 4.0 or later.

- **AllowLateScanning.** Allowed values are 0 or 1. If set to 1, UrlScan registers itself as a low priority filter. This allows other filters to modify the URL before UrlScan does its analysis (note that in addition to this switch, it is necessary to ensure that UrlScan is listed lower on the filter list than the high priority filters in the MMC ISAPI Filters property sheet for the server). If this value is set to the default value of 0, UrlScan runs as a high priority filter. Note that FrontPage Server Extensions require that this setting be 1 and that UrlScan is low on the filter load order list, preferably last.

- **PerDayLogging.** Allowed values are 0 or 1. If set to the default value of 1, UrlScan creates a new log file each day and appends a date to the log file name (for example, UrlScan.101501.log). If both PerDayLogging=1 and PerProcessLogging=1 are set, the log file name contains the date and a process ID in the name (for example, UrlScan.101501.123.log). Note that with PerDayLogging, a log is be created for the current day (and the log for the previous day is closed) when the first log entry is written for that day. If a day passes with no UrlScan activity, no log is created for that day. If this value is set to 0, then UrlScan opens a single file called UrlScan.log (or UrlScan.xxx.log, where xxx is the process ID, in the case of PerProcessLogging=1).

- **RejectResponseUrl.** Allowed value is a string. The default is /<Rejected-By-UrlScan>. This string is a URL in the form: /path/file_name.ext. In the event UrlScan rejects a request, it will run the specified URL, which needs to be local to the Web site for the request being analyzed by UrlScan. The specified URL can have the same extension (for example, .asp) as the rejected URL.

- **UseFastPathReject.** Allowed values are 0 or 1. If set to 1, UrlScan ignores the RejectResponseUrl and returns a short 404 response to the client in cases where it rejects a request. This is faster than allowing the full processing of the RejectResponseUrl, but if this option is used, IIS cannot return a custom 404 response or log many parts of the request into the IIS log (the UrlScan log file will still contain complete information about rejected requests). The default is to not enable UseFastPathReject

The [AllowVerbs] section contains a list of HTTP verbs (methods). If UseAllowVerbs is set to 1 in the [Options] section, UrlScan rejects any request containing a verb not explicitly listed here. The entries in this section are case sensitive.

The [DenyVerbs] section contains a list of HTTP verbs (methods). If UseAllowVerbs is set to 0 in the [Options] section, UrlScan rejects any request containing a verb that is listed here. The entries in this section are case insensitive.

The [DenyHeaders] section contains a list of request headers that, if included in a received request, will be rejected. The entries in this section are case insensitive.

The [AllowExtensions] section contains a list of file extensions. If UseAllowExtensions is set to 1 in the [Options] section, any request containing a URL with an extension not explicitly listed here is rejected. The entries in this section are case insensitive.

Note: You can specify extensionless requests (for example, requests for a default page or a directory listing) by adding an empty extension using a dot and no trailing characters.

The [DenyExtensions] section contains a list of file extensions. If UseAllowExtensions is set to 0 in the [Options] section, any request containing a URL with an extension listed here is rejected. The entries in this section are case insensitive.

Note: If you make changes to the UrlScan.ini file you must restart ISA PROXY3 service to insure that ISAPI filter gets reloaded.

Network Scanning Using UrlScan with ISA Server

When deploying UrlScan on a ISA Server at the network perimeter, you must ensure that the UrlScan.ini settings allow all traffic required by Web servers behind the ISA Server to pass through. This may require manual configuration of the UrlScan.ini file.

When defining UrlScan.ini settings at an ISA Server, as a first step you should document all Web publishing rules configured at the ISA Server. These rules define exactly what HTTP and HTTPS traffic will pass through the ISA Server.

Once all Web traffic is identified, you should profile the Web traffic to enable the configuration of the UrlScan.ini file. When you define the settings, remember that the perimeter intrusion detection must allow all required traffic to pass. If there are conflicts between the security configurations of two Web servers, the least restrictive settings must be deployed at the network perimeter. For example, if you have two Web servers protected by an ISA Server, and one Web server hosts an ASP-based Web site, while the second Web server only hosts static content, UrlScan deployed at the ISA Server must allow ASP-related traffic to pass to both Web servers. You can further lock down the traffic at the Web server hosting static content by implementing UrlScan at that Web server.

End Point Scanning Using UrlScan with IIS

You can define specific UrlScan.ini settings to meet the requirements of the individual Web servers.

URLScan is useful in protecting Web servers because many attacks share a common characteristic—they involve the use of an unusual request. For example, the request might be extremely long, request an unusual action, be encoded using an alternate character set, or include character sequences that are rarely seen in legitimate requests. By filtering out all unusual requests, URLScan prevents them from reaching the server and potentially causing damage.

URLScan is very flexible. Its default rule set fully protects a server against virtually all known security vulnerabilities affecting IIS, as well as potentially protecting against additional, as yet undiscovered attack methods. The default rules can be modified—and new rules can be added—in order to customize the tool's actions to match the needs of a particular server. In addition to the default rule set, the following configurations can be selected in the IIS LockDown wizard during the installation of the UrlScan.ini ISAPI filter:

- Small Business Server 2000
- Exchange Server 5.5 (Outlook Web Access)

- Exchange Server 2000 (OWA, PF Management, IM, SMTP, NNTP)
- SharePoint Portal Server
- FrontPage Server Extensions (SharePoint Team Services)
- BizTalk Server 2000
- Commerce Server 2000
- Proxy Server
- Static Web Server
- Dynamic Web server (ASP Enabled)
- Other (Server that does not match any of the listed roles)
- Server that does not require IIS

When you select one of the preconfigured templates, a predefined UrlScan.ini file is deployed with the optimal settings. In addition to accepting the prescribed UrlScan.ini file, ensure that you search the latest Microsoft Knowledge Base articles for any adjustments required to the Urlscan.ini file for specific configurations.

Specific UrlScan Configuration Recommendations

Several Knowledge Base articles exist that provide recommended configuration settings when using UrlScan in specific environments. When researching UrlScan configuration settings, be sure to review the following articles:

Q309394: HOW TO: Use URLScan with FrontPage 2000

Q309508: IIS Lockdown and URLscan Configurations in Exchange Environment

Q309677: XADM: Known Issues and Fine Turning When You Use the IIS Lockdown Wizard in an Exchange 2000 Environment

Q311595: XCCC: How to Install and Configure Microsoft Security Tool Kit On a Microsoft Mobile Information Server

Q312376: HOW TO: Configure URLScan to Allow Requests with a Null Extension in IIS

Q313131: HOW TO: Use URLScan with Exchange Outlook Web Access in Exchange Server 5.5

Q311862: How to Use The IIS Lockdown Tool with Small Business Server

Q311350: HOW TO: Create a Custom Server Type for Use with the IIS Lockdown Wizard

Intrusion Detection Features of ISA Server

ISA Server features an integrated intrusion detection system, which can determine when an attack is attempted against your network and respond with a set of pre-configured actions, or *alerts*. To detect unwanted intrusion, ISA Server compares network traffic and log entries to well known attack methods. Suspicious activities trigger alerts, which cause ISA Server to execute a number of actions. Possible actions include running a program, sending an e-mail message, logging the event in the Windows event log, stopping and starting ISA Server services, or any combination of these.

When intrusion detection is enabled, alerts can be configured for the following attacks:

- **All Port Scan.** A method used by attackers to determine the open ports on a target computer or network. The intrusion detection engine detects multiple attempts to connect to ports and sends an alert when the number of connection attempts is greater than an administrator configured threshold. ISA Server can also be configured to detect port scanning on well known ports only (1-2048).

- **IP Half Scan.** This attack is similar to the All Port Scan, but takes advantage of the fact that TCP communication is a three-step process. An IP Half Scan does not send the third packet of the TCP three-way handshake to avoid detection.

- **Land Attack.** A packet with a spoofed source IP address and port number that matches that of the destination address and port is sent to a computer. The spoofed packet causes the target computer to enter a loop that eventually crashes it.

- **Ping of Death.** This attack involves a large number of exceptionally large ICMP echo request (ping) packets being sent to a single computer. The target computer tries to respond to all of the packets, causing a buffer overflow that crashes the computer.

- **UDP Bomb.** A UDP packet that is constructed with illegal values in certain fields will cause some older operating systems to crash when the packet is received. If the target computer crashes, it is often difficult to determine the cause.

- **Windows Out-of-Band.** Also known as *WinNuke*, this is a denial of service attack which can be used to disable Windows networks. A successful attack causes loss of network connectivity or a crash on vulnerable computers.

Additional intrusion detection functionality is available from ISA Server third-party partners or can be created using the application filters interfaces in the ISA Server Software Development Kit. For further details, see the "More Information" section at the end of this chapter.

Note: Intrusion attempt alerts can be viewed in the ISA Server management console in the Internet Security and Acceleration Server\Servers and Arrays\<*ServerName*>\Monitoring \Alerts folder.

Third-party Solutions for Intrusion Detection

Third-party solutions exist for both network and end point intrusion detection systems. These third-party solutions provide support for protocols other than HTTP and also scan for well known attacks against networked computers.

The common types of attacks that intrusion detection systems should identify include:

- **Reconnaisance attacks.** These occur when an intruder is staking out a network, looking for vulnerabilities. Potential attacks include ping sweeps, DNS zone transfers, e-mail reconnaissance, port scans, and download of Web site content to look for vulnerable scripts and sample pages.

- **Exploit attacks.** These occur when Intruders take advantage of hidden features or bugs to gain access to the system. Most often, the attack points were identified by a previous exploit attack.

- **Denial of service (DoS) attacks.** These occur when an intruder attempts to crash a service running on a machine by overloading a resource, such as network links, the CPU, or the disk subsystem. The intruder is not trying to gain information, but to is attempting to disable your computer from usage.

A good intrusion detection system should be able to identify all three forms of attacks. Two different methods are used to identify attacks:

- **Anomaly detection.** Based on taking a baseline of a computer on the network. Deviations from the baseline can identify an intrusion attempt. For example, an increase in logon attempts at off-peak hours can identify a compromised computer. The advantage of anomaly detection, is that it can identify attacks without understanding exactly how the attack takes place.

- **Signature recognition.** Identifies attacks based on the well known patterns of the attacks. For example, many Web server attacks use common patterns that are easily identifiable. By comparing incoming application traffic to signature strings in a database, an instruction detection system can identify these attacks. The disadvantage of this method of intrusion detection system is that the signature database must be frequently be updated to identify new attack signatures.

Some of the third party products available for testing and deployment include:

- **BlackIce Defender** (http://www.iss.net/products_services/hsoffice_protection/)
- **CyberCop Scanner** (http://www.pgp.com/products/cybercop-scanner/default.asp)
- **ICEpac Security Suite** (www.networkice.com/products/icepac_suite.html)
- **Cisco Secure IDS** (http://www.cisco.com/warp/public/cc/pd/sqsw/sqidsz/prodlit/netra_ds.htm)

- **eTrust Intrusion Detection** (http://www3.ca.com/Solutions/Product.asp?ID=163)
- **Snort** (www.snort.org)
- **Tripwire** (www.tripwiresecurity.com)
- **Foundstone Attacker** (www.foundstone.com)

Vulnerability Assessment

In addition to performing passive and active intrusion detection, you should also perform periodic vulnerability assessments. Vulnerability assessments simulate an attack on your network and detect the vulnerabilities that an attacker would find.

By performing periodic assessments you can find vulnerabilities before an attacker does and secure the weakened portion of your network to protect against the vulnerability.

When researching vulnerability assessment tools, include the following requirements in your decision making process:

- **Database Update Mechanism.** The tool should provide an automated method to update the signatures for vulnerabilities so that the tool is not out of date after a short period of time.
- **Minimize False Positives.** The tool should filter out false positives so that an organization does not waste time investigating nonsecurity events.
- **Ability to store results in a database.** The tool should allow archiving of scan results to perform trend analysis and detect changes in security over time.
- **Provide solutions to found vulnerabilities.** If a vulnerability is found, the tool should provide documentation on how to fix the vulnerability or provide scripts that perform the tasks to protect against the vulnerability.

Several third-party tools exist to perform vulnerability assessments against a Windows 2000 network. These tools include:

- Symantec NetRecon 3.5 (enterprisesecurity.symantec.com)
- BindView Security Advisor (www.bindview.com)
- eEye Digital Security. Retina Network Security Scanner (http://www.eeye.com)
- Internet Security Systems (ISS) Internet Scanner (www.iss.net)
- Network Associates CyberCop (www.pgp.com/products/default.asp)

Alternatively, it may be more appropriate to bring in a third-party consulting service to perform the vulnerability assessment. The advantage of using a third party service is that they have no previous knowledge of the network and will be working from the same starting point as an external attacker. Many times, these external assessments will provide the most useful information, based on the neutrality of the assessment team.

Summary

Auditing and Intrusion Detection is a major part of effective defense in your environment. As part of your risk management process, you should determine how much auditing and intrusion detection is appropriate for your environment. For Intrusion detection across multiple protocols, you may wish to consider third-party tools.

More Information

For more information from Symantec on auditing and intrusion detection, see:

http://securityresponse.symantec.com/avcenter/security/Content/security.articles /ids.and.auditing.html

External time servers:

ntp2.usno.navy.mil and tock.usno.navy.mil

ISA Server Partners Information:

http://www.microsoft.com/isaserver/partners

ISA Server Solution Developers Kit (SDK):

http://www.microsoft.com/isaserver/techinfo/productdoc/2000/SDKdownload.asp

Writing Secure Code by Michael Howard and David LeBlanc (Microsoft Press; ISBN: 0-7356-1588-8)

7

Responding to Incidents

How prepared is your IT department to handle a security incident? Many organizations only learn how to respond to a security incident after suffering an attack. By this time the incident may have proved much more costly than is necessary. Proper incident response should be an integral part of your overall security policy and risk mitigation strategy.

There are clearly direct benefits in responding to security incidents. However, there may also be indirect financial benefits. For example, your insurance company may offer discounts if you can demonstrate your organization is normally able to quickly and cost-effectively handle attacks. Or, if you are a service provider, a formal incident response plan might help win business because it shows that you take seriously the process of good information security.

Minimizing the Number and Severity of Security Incidents

In most areas of life, prevention is better than cure, and security is no exception. Wherever possible, you will want to prevent security incidents from happening in the first place. However it is impossible to prevent all security incidents, so when a security incident does happen, you will need to ensure that its impact is minimal. There are prudent measures you can take to minimize the number and impact of security incidents. These include:

- Clearly establishing and enforcing all policies and procedures. Many security incidents are accidentally created by IT personnel who have not followed or understood change management procedures or have improperly configured security devices, such as firewalls and authentication systems. Your policies and procedures should be thoroughly tested to ensure that they are practical, clear and provide the appropriate level of security.

- Gaining management support for security policies and incident handling.

- Routinely monitoring and analyzing network traffic and system performance.
- Routinely checking all logs and logging mechanisms. These would include operating system event logs, application specific logs and intrusion detection system logs.
- Routinely assessing for vulnerabilities in your environment. This should be done by a security specialist with special clearance to perform these actions.
- Routinely checking servers to ensure they have all of the latest patches installed.
- Establishing security training programs for both IT staff and end users. The largest vulnerability in any system is the naïve user—the ILOVEYOU worm effectively exploited that vulnerability.
- Posting security banners that remind users of their responsibilities and restrictions, along with a warning of potential prosecution for violation. Without such banners it may be difficult or impossible to prosecute offenders. You should obtain legal advice to ensure that the wording of your security banners is appropriate.
- Developing, implementing, and enforcing a policy requiring complex passwords.
- Verifying your back up and restore procedures. You should be aware of where backups are maintained, who can access them, and your procedures for data restoration and system recovery. Make sure that you regularly verify backups and media by selectively restoring data.
- Creating a Computer Security Incident Response Team (CSIRT). This is a group of people with responsibilities for dealing with any security incident. Your CSIRT should consist of members whose duties are clearly defined to ensure that no area is left uncovered in your response (more details on assembling a CSIRT can be found later in this chapter).
- Training information security members of your CSIRT on proper use and location of critical security tools. You should consider providing laptops preconfigured with these tools to ensure that no time is wasted installing and configuring tools to respond to an incident. These systems and the associated tools must be properly protected when not in use.
- Assembling all relevant communication information. You should ensure that you have contact names and phone numbers for people within your organization that need to be notified (including members of the CSIRT, those responsible for supporting all of your systems, and those in charge of media relations). You will also need details for your ISP and local and national law enforcement agencies. Consider contacting local law enforcement before an incident happens. This will help you ensure you understand proper procedures for communicating incidents and collecting evidence.

- Placing all emergency system information in a central, offline location, such as a physical notebook, or an offline computer. This emergency information includes passwords to systems, IP addresses, router configuration information, firewall rule set lists, copies of certificate authority keys, contact names and phone numbers, escalation procedures, and so on. This information must both be kept extremely physically secure and readily available. One method of securing and making readily available is to encrypt the information on a dedicated security laptop placed in a secure vault and limiting access to authorized individuals such as the CSIRT leader and Chief Information Officer or Chief Technology Officer.

Assembling the Core Computer Security Incident Response Team

The CSIRT is the focal point for dealing with computer security incidents in your environment. Its responsibilities include:

- Monitoring systems for security breaches.
- Serving as a central communication point, both to receive reports of security incidents and to disseminate vital information to appropriate entities about the incident.
- Documenting and cataloging security incidents.
- Promoting security awareness within the company to help prevent incidents from occurring in your organization.
- Supporting system and network auditing through processes such as vulnerability assessment and penetration testing.
- Keeping up with new vulnerabilities and attack strategies employed by attackers.
- Keeping up with new software patches.
- Analyzing and develop new technologies for minimizing security vulnerabilities and risks.
- Providing security consulting services.
- Continually honing and updating current systems and procedures.

The ideal CSIRT membership and structure depends on the type of your organization and your risk management strategy, however, the CSIRT should generally form part or all of your organizations' security team. Inside the core team are security professionals responsible for coordinating a response to any incident. The number of members in the CSIRT will typically depend upon the size and complexity of your organization. However, you should ensure that there are enough members to adequately cover all the duties of the team at any time.

CSIRT Team Leader

It is important that the CSIRT has an individual responsible for its activities. The CSIRT Team Leader will generally be responsible for the activities of the CSIRT and will coordinate reviews of its actions. This may lead to changes in polices and procedures for dealing with future incidents.

CSIRT Incident Lead

In the event of an incident, there should be one individual responsible for coordinating the response. The CSIRT Incident Lead has ownership of the particular incident or set of related security incidents. All communication about the event is coordinated through the Incident Lead and when speaking with those outside the CSIRT, he or she represents the entire CSIRT. The Incident Lead may differ depending on the nature of the incident and is often different to the CSIRT Team Leader.

CSIRT Associate Members

As well as your core CSIRT team, you should have a number of specific individuals who handle and respond to particular incidents. Associate members will come from a variety of different departments in your organization, and specialize in areas that are affected by security incidents but would not be dealt with directly by the core CSIRT. Associate members may either be directly involved in an incident or be an entry point to delegate responsibility to a more appropriate individual within their department. The table shows some suggested associate members and their roles.

Table 7.1: CSIRT Associate Members

Associate Member	Description of Role
IT Contact	Primary responsibility for coordinating communication between the CSIRT Incident Lead and the rest of the IT group. This person may not have the particular technical expertise to respond to the incident at hand, however they will be primarily responsible for finding people in the IT group to handle particular security events.
Legal Representative	Typically a member of the in-house legal staff and very familiar with established incident response policies. The legal representative determines how to proceed during an incident with minimal legal liability and maximum ability to prosecute offenders. Before an incident occurs, the legal representative should have input on monitoring and response policies to ensure the organization is not being put at legal risk during a cleanup or containment operation. It is imperative to consider the legal implications of shutting down a system and potentially violating service level agreements or membership agreements with your customers or not shutting down a compromised system and being liable for damages caused by attacks launched from that system. Any communication to outside law enforcement or external investigative agencies should also be coordinated with the legal representative.

Associate Member	Description of Role
Communications Officer	Generally a member of the public relations department, this individual is responsible for protecting and promoting the image of the organization. They may not be the actual face to the media and customers, but they are responsible for crafting the message (while the content and objective of the message is generally the responsibility of management). All media inquiries should be directed to the communications officer.
Management	Management involvement may be anything between departmental and organization-wide. The appropriate management individual will vary according to the impact, location, severity, and type of incident. If you have a managerial point of contact, you can quickly identify the most appropriate individual for the specific circumstances. Management is responsible for approving and directing security policy. They are also responsible for determining the total impact (both financial and otherwise) of the incident upon the organization. Management directs the communications officer regarding which information should be disclosed to the media and determines the level of interaction between the legal representative and law enforcement agencies.

How the CSIRT Responds to an Incident

In the event of an incident, the CSIRT will coordinate a response from the core CSIRT, and will communicate with the associate members of the CSIRT. The following table shows the responsibilities of these individuals during the incident response process.

Table 7.2: Responsibilities of CSIRT During the Incident Response Process

Activities	Roles				
	CSIRT Incident Lead	IT Contact	Legal Representative	Communications Officer	Management
Initial Assessment	Owner	Advises	None	None	None
Initial Response	Owner	Implements	Updated	Updated	Updated
Collects Forensic Evidence	Implements	Advises	Owner	None	None
Implements Temporary Fix	Owner	Implements	Updated	Updated	Advises

(continued)

Activities	Roles				
	CSIRT Incident Lead	IT Contact	Legal Representative	Communications Officer	Management
Sends Communication	Advisor	Advises	Advises	Implements	Owner
Check with Local Law Enforcement	Updater	Updated	Implements	Updated	Owner
Implements Permanent Fix	Owner	Implements	Updated	Updated	Updated
Determines Financial Impact on Business	Updater	Updated	Advises	Updated	Owner

Defining an Incident Response Plan

All members of your IT environment should be aware of what to do in the event of an incident. While the CSIRT will perform most actions in response to an incident, all levels of your IT staff should be aware of how to report incidents internally. End users should report suspicious activity to the IT staff directly or through a help desk rather than directly to the CSIRT.

The incident response plan should be reviewed in detail by all team members and easily accessible to all IT staff. This will help to ensure that when an incident does occur, the right procedures are followed.

Your incident response plan should include these steps:

- Making an initial assessment
- Communicating the incident
- Containing the damage/minimizing the risk
- Identifying the type and severity of the compromise
- Protecting evidence
- Notifying external agencies
- Recovering systems
- Compiling and organizing incident documentation
- Assessing incident damage and cost
- Reviewing the response and updating policies

Note: Job Aid 4: Incident Response Quick Reference Card can be used during an incident as a checklist to ensure that all phases are properly executed.

These steps are not purely sequential. Rather they happen throughout the incident. For example, documentation starts at the very beginning and continues throughout the entire life cycle of the incident, communication also happens throughout the entire incident.

Other aspects of the process will work alongside each other. For example, as part of your initial assessment, you will gain an idea of the general nature of the attack. It is important to use this information to contain the damage and minimize risk as soon as possible. If you act quickly, you can help to save time, money and your organization's reputation. However, until you understand in more detail the type and severity of the compromise, you will not be able to be really effective in containing the damage and minimizing the risk. An over zealous response could even cause more damage than the initial attack. By working these two steps alongside each other, you will get the best compromise between swift and effective action.

Note: It is very important that you thoroughly test your incident response process before an incident occurs. Without thorough testing, you cannot be confident that the measures you have in place will be effective in responding to incidents.

Making an Initial Assessment

Many activities could indicate a possible attack in your organization. For example, a network administrator performing legitimate system maintenance will appear similar to someone launching some form of attack. In other cases, a badly configured system may lead to a number of false positives in an intrusion detection system, making it more difficult to spot genuine incidents.

As part of your initial assessment you should:

- Take initial steps to determine if you are dealing with an actual incident or a false positive.
- Gain a general idea of the type and severity of attack. This should be at least enough information to begin communicating it for further research and to begin containing the damage and minimizing the risk.
- Record your actions thoroughly. These records will later be used for documenting the incident (whether actual or false).

Note: While you would like to avoid false positives as much as possible, it is always better to act on a false positive than fail to act on a genuine incident. Your initial assessment should therefore be as brief as possible, yet still eliminate obvious false positives.

Communicate the Incident

Once you suspect that there is a security incident, you should quickly communicate the breach to the rest of the core CSIRT. The incident lead, along with the rest of the team should quickly identify who needs to be contacted outside of the core CSIRT. This will help to ensure that appropriate control and coordination of the incident can be maintained while minimizing the extent of the damage. Be aware that damage can come in many forms and that a headline in the newspaper describing a security breach can be much more destructive than many system intrusions. For this reason and to prevent an attacker from being tipped off, only those playing a role in the incident response should be informed until it is properly controlled. Based upon the situation, your team will later determine who needs to be informed on the incident. This could be anything from specific individuals up to the entire company and external customers.

Contain the Damage and Minimize the Risk

By acting quickly to reduce the actual and potential effects of an attack you can make the difference between a minor and a major event. RFC 2196 defines a series of priorities for containing damage in your environment. The exact response will depend on your organization and the nature of the attack you face. However, the following priorities are suggested as a starting point.

1. **Protect human life and people's safety.** This should, of course, always be your first priority.

2. **Protect classified and/or sensitive data.** As part of your planning for incident response, you should clearly define which data is classified and sensitive. This will allow you to prioritize your responses in protecting the data.

3. **Protect other data, including proprietary, scientific and managerial data.** Other data in your environment may still be of great value. You should act to protect the most valuable data first, before moving on to other, less useful data.

4. **Protect hardware and software against attack.** This would include protecting against loss or alteration of system files and physical damage to hardware. Damage to systems can result in costly downtime.

5. **Minimize disruption of computing resources (including processes).** Although uptime is very important in most environments, keeping systems up during an attack may result in greater problems later on. For this reason, minimizing disruption of computing resources should generally be a relatively low priority.

There are a number of measures you can take to contain the damage and minimize the risk to your environment. As a minimum, you should:

- Try to avoid letting attackers know that you are aware of their activities. This can be difficult, because some essential responses may alert attackers. For example, if there is an emergency meeting of the CSIRT, or you require an immediate change of all passwords, any internal attackers may know that you are aware of an incident.

- Compare the cost of taking the compromised and related systems offline against the risk of continuing operations. In the vast majority of cases you should immediately take the system off the network. However, there may be service agreements in place that may require keeping systems available even with the possibility of further damage occurring. Under these circumstances, you may choose to keep a system online with limited connectivity in order to gather additional evidence during an ongoing attack.

  In some cases, the damage and scope of an incident may be so extensive that you may have to take action which invokes the penalty clauses specified in your service level agreements. In any case, it is very important that the actions you will take in the event of an incident are discussed in advance and outlined in your response plan so that immediate action can be taken when an attack occurs.

- Determine the access point(s) used by the attacker and implement measures to prevent future access. Measures may include disabling a modem, adding access control entries to a router or firewall, or increasing physical security measures.

- Consider rebuilding a fresh system with new hard disks (the existing hard disks should be removed and put in storage as these may be used as evidence if you decide to prosecute attackers). Ensure that any local passwords are different than before the attack. You should also change administrative and service account passwords elsewhere in your environment.

Identify the Severity of the Compromise

To be able to recover effectively from attack, you need to determine how seriously your systems have been compromised. This will determine how to further contain and minimize the risk, how to recover, how quickly and to whom you communicate the incident, and whether or not to seek legal redress.

You should attempt to:

- Determine the nature of the attack (this may be different than the initial assessment suggests).
- Determine the attack point of origin.
- Determine the intent of the attack. Was the attack specifically directed at your organization to acquire specific information or was it a random attack?
- Identify the systems that have been compromised.
- Identify the files that have been accessed and determine the sensitivity of those files.

By performing these actions, you will be able to determine the appropriate responses for your environment. A good incident response plan will outline specific procedures to follow as you learn more about the attack. Generally the nature of the attack symptoms will determine the order in which you follow the procedures defined in your plan. As time is crucial, less time consuming procedures should generally be followed before more lengthy procedures. To help you determine the severity of the compromise you should:

- Contact other members of the response team to inform them of your findings, have them verify your results, determine if they are aware of related activity or other potential attack activity, and to help identify whether the incident is a false positive. In some cases, what appeared to be a genuine incident on initial assessment will prove to be a false positive.

- Determine if unauthorized hardware has been attached to the network or if there are any signs of unauthorized access through the compromise of physical security controls.

- Examine key groups (Domain Administrators, Administrators, and so on) for unauthorized entries.

- Search for security assessment or exploitation software. Cracking utilities are often found on compromised systems during evidence gathering.

- Look for unauthorized processes or applications currently running or set to run using the startup folders or registry entries.

- Search for gaps in, or absence of, system logs.

- Review intrusion detection system logs for signs of intrusion, which systems may have been affected, methods of attack, time and length of attack, and potentially the overall extent of damage.

- Examine other log files for unusual connections, security audit failures, unusual security audit successes, failed logon attempts, attempts to log on to default accounts, activity during nonworking hours, file, directory and share permission changes, and elevated or changed user permissions.

- Compare systems to previously conducted file/system integrity checks. This allows you to identify additions, deletions, modifications, and permission and control modifications to the file system and registry. A great deal of time can be saved when responding to incidents if you identify exactly what has been compromised and what areas need to be recovered.

- Search for sensitive data such as credit card numbers and employee or customer data that may have been moved or hidden for future retrieval/modifications. Systems may also need to be checked for nonbusiness data, such as pornography (unless you're in the pornography business), illegal copies of software, and e-mail or other records that may assist in an investigation. If there is a possibility of violating privacy or other laws by searching on a system for investigative purposes, you should contact your legal department before you proceed.

- Match the performance of suspected systems against their baseline performance levels. This of course presupposes that baselines have been created and properly updated. For more information on creating a performance baseline, see Chapter 27 of the *Windows 2000 Professional Resource Kit* (Microsoft Press; ISBN: 1-57231-808-2), "Overview of Performance Monitoring."

When determining which systems have been compromised and how, you will generally be comparing your systems against a previously recorded baseline of the same system before it was compromised. Assuming that a recent system snapshot is sufficient for comparison may put you in a difficult situation if the previous snapshot comes from a system which has already been attacked.

Note: Tools such as EventCombMT, DumpEL and Microsoft Operations Manager can help you determine how much a system has been attacked. Third-party intrusion detection systems give advance warning of attacks and other tools will show file changes on your systems. For more information on these tools, see Chapter 6, "Auditing and Intrusion Detection."

Protect Evidence

In many cases, if your environment has been deliberately attacked, you will want to take legal action against the perpetrators. If you are going to do this, you will need to gather evidence that can be used against them. It is extremely important to backup the compromised systems as soon as possible, and prior to performing any actions that could affect data integrity on the original media. You should get someone skilled in computer forensics to make at least two complete bit-for-bit backups of the entire system using new, never before used media. At least one backup should be on a write once, read many media such as a CD-R or DVD-R. This backup should only be used for prosecution of the offender and should be physically secured until needed. The other backup may be used for data recovery. These backups should not be accessed except for legal purposes, so you should physically secure them. You will also need to document information about the backups, such as who backed up the systems, at what time, how they were secured and anyone who had access to them.

Once the back ups are performed, you should remove the original hard drives and store them in a physically secure location. These can be used as forensic evidence in the event of a prosecution. New hard disks should be used to restore the system.

In some cases the benefit of preserving data may not equal the cost of delaying the response and recovery of the system. The costs and benefits of preserving data should be compared to those of faster recovery for each event.

For extremely large systems, comprehensive back ups of all compromised systems may not be feasible. Instead you should back up all logs and selected, breached, portions of the system.

If possible, back up system state as well. It may be months or years until prosecution takes place, so it is important to have as much detail of the incident archived for future use.

Often the most difficult legal aspect of prosecuting a cyber crime is collecting evidence in a manner acceptable to the particular jurisdiction's laws of evidence submission. Hence, the most critical component to the forensic process is detailed and complete documentation of how systems were handled, by whom, and when, in order to demonstrate reliable evidence. Sign and date every page of the documentation.

Once you have working, verified backups, you can wipe the infected systems and rebuild them. This gets you back up and running quickly. It is the backups that provide the critical, untainted evidence required for prosecution. A backup separate from the forensic backup should be used to restore data.

Notify External Agencies

After the incident has been contained and data preserved for potential prosecution, you will need to start notifying appropriate external entities. Potential agencies include local and national law enforcement, external security agencies, and virus experts. External agencies can provide technical assistance, offering faster resolution and providing information learned from similar incidents to help you fully recover from the incident and prevent it from occurring in the future.

For particular industries and types of breaches, it may be necessary to specifically notify customers and/or the general public, particularly if customers may be affected directly by the incident.

If the event caused substantial financial impact, you may need to report the incident to law enforcement agencies.

For higher profile companies and incidents, there may be media involvement. While media attention to a security incident is never desirable, it is often unavoidable and more beneficial to the company to take a proactive stance in communicating the incident. At a minimum, the incident response procedures should clearly define the individuals authorized to speak to media representatives. Normally these will be people in the public relations group within your organization. You should not attempt to deny to the media that an incident has occurred as doing so is more likely to damage your reputation more than proactive admissions and visible responses ever will. This does not mean that the media should be notified for each and every incident regardless of its nature or severity. You should assess the appropriate media response on a case by case basis.

Recover Systems

How you recover your system will generally depend on the extent of the security breach. You will need to determine whether you can restore the existing system leaving intact as much as possible, or if it is necessary to completely rebuild the system.

Restoring data presumes, of course, that you have clean backups—backups made *before* the incident occurred. File integrity software can help pinpoint the first occurrence of damage. If the software alerts you to a changed file, then you know that the backup you made just before the alert is a good one and should be preserved for use when rebuilding the compromised system.

An incident could potentially corrupt data for many months prior to discovery. It is therefore very important that as part of your incident response process, you determine the duration of the incident. (File/system integrity software and intrusion detection systems can assist you in this.) In some cases the latest or even several backups prior may not be long enough to get to a clean state, so you would be advised to regularly archive data backups in a secure offsite location.

Compile and Organize Incident Documentation

The CSIRT should thoroughly document all processes as they deal with any incident. This should include a description of the breach and details of each action taken (who took the action, when they took it and the reasoning behind it). All people involved and with access must be noted throughout the response process. The documentation should be chronologically organized, checked for completeness, signed and reviewed with management and legal representatives. You will also need to safeguard the evidence collected in the protect evidence phase. You should consider having two people present during all phases and who can sign off on each step. This will help reduce the likelihood of evidence being inadmissible and reduce the possibility of evidence being modified after the fact.

Remember that the offender may be an employee, contractor, temporary employee or other insider within your organization. Without thorough, detailed documentation, identifying an inside offender will be very difficult. Proper documentation also gives you the best chance of prosecuting offenders.

Assess Incident Damage and Cost

When determining the damage to your organization, you should consider both direct and indirect costs. These would include:

- Costs due to the loss of competitive edge from the release of proprietary or sensitive information
- Legal costs

- Labor costs to analyze the breaches, reinstall software and recover data
- Costs relating to system downtime (for example, lost employee productivity, lost sales, replacement of hardware, software and other property)
- Costs of repairing and possibly updating damaged or ineffective physical security measures (locks, walls, cages, and so on)
- Other consequential damages such as loss of reputation or customer trust

Review Response and Update Policies

Once the documentation phase and recovery phase are complete you should review the process thoroughly. Determine with your team the steps that were executed successfully and what mistakes were made. In some cases you will find that your processes need to be modified to allow you to handle incidents better in the future.

Case Study – Northwind Traders Incident Handling

To see how the different stages of incident response should work to deal with an attack, we have designed a case study, showing the response of the Northwind Traders CSIRT team to an infection of the Code Red II worm. Although this case study is fictional, the measures taken closely mirror those taken by real organizations in the event of an attack.

Table 7.3: Northwind Traders Case Study

Incident Response Step	Action Taken
Make initial assessment	Samantha Smith an on-call CSIRT member, is paged with a brief description of an event logged by the Northwind Traders' intrusion detection system. The system indicates a possible Code Red II incident on the Web server, WEB2. She examines WEB2's IIS log file for the signature string and checks for the existence of root.exe on c:\inetpub\scripts. The results of these investigations strongly suggest that this is not a false positive.
Communicate the incident	Samantha notifies the rest of the CSIRT by telephone of the initial findings and agrees to follow up with additional details as soon as they are available.
Containing the damage and minimizing the risk	Northwind Traders' incident response policy states that verification of the presence of a worm requires the system being removed from the network. Samantha removes the network cable. Fortunately, WEB2 is part of a set of load-balanced servers, so customers will not experience downtime due to the disconnection.
Identify the severity of the compromise	Samantha scans the log files of other servers to determine if the worm has spread. She discovers that it has not.

Incident Response Step	Action Taken
Communicate the incident	Samantha communicates these findings to the rest of the CSIRT by e-mail and directly contacts the CSIRT leader. The CSIRT leader designates Mike Danseglio, an Information Security Manager, as Incident Lead. Mike will coordinate all activity and communication to and from the core CSIRT. Mike notifies the Director of Technology and the on-call Information Technology team that the Web server has been disconnected from the network and that it will be cleaned of the worm before it is reconnected again. Mike also notifies the executive management, the communications officer and the legal representative. The legal representative informs Mike that although prosecution may not be possible, they would still rather he follow procedures to collect evidence.
Contain the damage and minimize the risk	Another CSIRT member, Robert Brown, runs Hfnetchk to determine if other servers have been patched for Code Red II. He finds that two other servers are not up to date and immediately applies the patch.
Identify the severity of the compromise	Robert, makes a further scan of log files of all other IIS servers, and determines no other instances of Code Red II exist at this time.
Protect evidence	Every indication is the damage has been contained to WEB2. Since the damage has been reasonably contained and legal has indicated that he should collect evidence, Mike decides to do this before performing a more intrusive analysis of the system that could disturb or destroy the evidence. Other team members continue to monitor the other Web servers and log for suspicious activity. A member of the CSIRT trained to collect forensic evidence creates two snapshots of the compromised system. One snapshot is carefully preserved for later forensic examination. The other snap-shot will potentially be used in the recovery process in conjunction with clean, secure backups prior to the event. The forensic backup is made from never before used write-once media, carefully documented, and sealed and secured along with the hard disks from the server, in accordance with security policy.
Identify the type and severity of the attack	The organizations security toolkit laptop, which contains a number of forensic tools, is used to review the recovery backup for indications of additional compromise. Registry entries and folders are reviewed for additions to areas that run software upon startup such as the profile/startup directories and Run and RunOnce registry keys. User and Groups accounts are reviewed as well along with User Rights and Security Policies for any modifications.

(continued)

Incident Response Step	Action Taken
Notify external agencies	Mike reports the incident to the FBI's National Infrastructure Protection Center, since Northwind Traders participates in many large U.S. government projects. Because neither customer information nor access to systems was compromised, customers are not notified.
Recover systems	Although there are tools to clean Code Red II from WEB2, the CSIRT and the WEB2 support team elect to reinstall the operating system to new media. By reinstalling the operating system from the original distribution and onto new media, they are ensured of having a clean system with no hacker backdoors or corrupted files. Once Windows 2000 is reinstalled, security is increased on the system by following the guidelines specified in the previous chapters of this guide. An uninfected backup is located and then, with great caution, data is restored. If data is only available from the compromised backup, it is restored to a separate, offline system and then reincorporated onto WEB2 after it is clear it does not pose a danger. The CSIRT team performs a complete vulnerability assessment of the system documenting all information discovered in the process. WEB2 is reconnected and closely monitored.
Compile and organize incident documentation	Mike and the CSIRT research the cause of the vulnerability and determine that the system was recently reinstalled and patches were not applied. This is against clearly defined policy already in place. The breakdown for this event occurred in three places: the Support team members failed to reapply the patches, the Information Security department failed to audit applied patches in a timely manner, and the Configuration Management group failed to identify the need to apply patches and then get Information Security involved in reviewing the system before returning to operational status. Any of these procedures would have prevented the incident. The team decides to implement a new procedure to prevent this incident from happening again. A checklist is created that must be completed by Change Management, Web Server Support, and Information Security prior to Information Security connecting or reconnecting any system to the internal network. The checklist procedure must be completed before Information Security will reconfigure the firewall to allow external access to and from this system. The Audit department should also regularly review that the checklists are being completed accurately and fully. Mike and the CSIRT compile all the documentation to determine what tasks were completed specific to the incident, the time each task took, and who performed them. This information is sent to the Finance representative to calculate the costs according the Generally Accepted Account Principles for computer damage. The CSIRT team leader ensures management understands the total cost of the event, why it occurred and how they plan to prevent it in the

Incident Response Step	Action Taken
	future. It is important for management to see the implications of not having or following procedures and not having resources, such as the CSIRT, in place.
	Overall incident documentation, lessons learned, and policies followed and not followed are reviewed by applicable team members.
	Documentation and procedures relevant to pursuing legal action are reviewed by the legal representative, the CSIRT team lead and incident lead, and executive management.

Summary

Much of this guide has dealt with measures you can take to minimize the risk of being attacked. However, a good way to handle security in your organization is to do everything you can to minimize your chances of attack, and then assume you will be. Part of this process is to audit carefully for attack, which is covered in Chapter 6. Another equally important part is to have a defined, well rehearsed, set of responses that you can put into place if a successful attack does occur.

Related Topics

Hacking Exposed Windows 2000 by Joel Scambray and Stuart McClure (McGraw-Hill Professional Publishing; ISBN: 0-0721-9262-3)

Computer Security Institute (www.gocsi.com)—releases an annual study called the Computer Crime and Security Survey

More Information

For more information from Symantec on incident response, see:

http://securityresponse.symantec.com/avcenter/security/Content/security.articles /incident.response.html

The *Handbook for Computer Security Incident Response Teams*:

http://interactive.sei.cmu.edu/Recent_Publications/1999/March/98hb001.htm

Forum of Incident Response and Security Teams (FIRST):

http://www.first.org

Incident Response: Investigating Computer Crime by Chris Prosise and Kevin Mandia (McGraw-Hill Professional Publishing; ISBN: 0-0721-3182-9)

The Internet Security Guidebook: From Planning to Deployment by Juanita Ellis, Tim Speed, William P. Crowell (Academic Pr; ISBN: 0-1223-7471-1)

RFC 2196:

http://www.ietf.org/rfc/rfc2196.txt?number=2196

Chapter 27 of the Windows 2000 Professional Resource Kit:

http://www.microsoft.com/technet/treeview/default.asp?url=/technet/prodtechnol/ windows2000pro/reskit/part6/proch27.asp

The Cert Coordination Center (CERT/CC):

http://www.cert.org

Appendix A

Additional Files Secured

Files secured by the Member Server Baseline Policy, in addition to the access control lists provided with the hisecws.inf template.

File	Baseline Permissions
%SystemDrive%\Boot.ini	Administrators: Full control System: Full control
%SystemDrive%\Ntdetect.com	Administrators: Full control System: Full control
%SystemDrive%\Ntldr	Administrators: Full control System: Full control
%SystemDrive%\Io.sys	Administrators: Full control System: Full control
%SystemDrive%\Autoexec.bat	Administrators: Full control System: Full control Authenticated Users: Read and Execute, List Folder Contents, and Read
%SystemDrive%\Config.sys	Administrators: Full control System: Full control Authenticated Users: Read and Execute, List Folder Contents, and Read
%SystemRoot%\system32\Append.exe	Administrators: Full control
%SystemRoot%\system32\Arp.exe	Administrators: Full control
%SystemRoot%\system32\At.exe	Administrators: Full control
%SystemRoot%\system32\Attrib.exe	Administrators: Full control
%SystemRoot%\system32\Cacls.exe	Administrators: Full control
%SystemRoot%\system32\Change.exe	Administrators: Full control
%SystemRoot%\system32\Chcp.com	Administrators: Full control

(continued)

File	Baseline Permissions
%SystemRoot%\system32\Chglogon.exe	Administrators: Full control
%SystemRoot%\system32\Chgport.exe	Administrators: Full control
%SystemRoot%\system32\Chguser.exe	Administrators: Full control
%SystemRoot%\system32\Chkdsk.exe	Administrators: Full control
%SystemRoot%\system32\Chkntfs.exe	Administrators: Full control
%SystemRoot%\system32\Cipher.exe	Administrators: Full control
%SystemRoot%\system32\Cluster.exe	Administrators: Full control
%SystemRoot%\system32\Cmd.exe	Administrators: Full control
%SystemRoot%\system32\Compact.exe	Administrators: Full control
%SystemRoot%\system32\Command.com	Administrators: Full control
%SystemRoot%\system32\Convert.exe	Administrators: Full control
%SystemRoot%\system32\Cscript.exe	Administrators: Full control
%SystemRoot%\system32\Debug.exe	Administrators: Full control
%SystemRoot%\system32\Dfscmd.exe	Administrators: Full control
%SystemRoot%\system32\Diskcomp.com	Administrators: Full control
%SystemRoot%\system32\Diskcopy.com	Administrators: Full control
%SystemRoot%\system32\Doskey.exe	Administrators: Full control
%SystemRoot%\system32\Edlin.exe	Administrators: Full control
%SystemRoot%\system32\Exe2bin.exe	Administrators: Full control
%SystemRoot%\system32\Expand.exe	Administrators: Full control
%SystemRoot%\system32\Fc.exe	Administrators: Full control
%SystemRoot%\system32\Find.exe	Administrators: Full control
%SystemRoot%\system32\Findstr.exe	Administrators: Full control
%SystemRoot%\system32\Finger.exe	Administrators: Full control
%SystemRoot%\system32\Forcedos.exe	Administrators: Full control
%SystemRoot%\system32\Format.com	Administrators: Full control
%SystemRoot%\system32\Ftp.exe	Administrators: Full control
%SystemRoot%\system32\Hostname.exe	Administrators: Full control
%SystemRoot%\system32\Iisreset.exe	Administrators: Full control
%SystemRoot%\system32\Ipconfig.exe	Administrators: Full control
%SystemRoot%\system32\Ipxroute.exe	Administrators: Full control
%SystemRoot%\system32\Label.exe	Administrators: Full control

File	Baseline Permissions
%SystemRoot%\system32\Logoff.exe	Administrators: Full control
%SystemRoot%\system32\Lpq.exe	Administrators: Full control
%SystemRoot%\system32\Lpr.exe	Administrators: Full control
%SystemRoot%\system32\Makecab.exe	Administrators: Full control
%SystemRoot%\system32\Mem.exe	Administrators: Full control
%SystemRoot%\system32\Mmc.exe	Administrators: Full control
%SystemRoot%\system32\Mode.com	Administrators: Full control
%SystemRoot%\system32\More.com	Administrators: Full control
%SystemRoot%\system32\Mountvol.exe	Administrators: Full control
%SystemRoot%\system32\Msg.exe	Administrators: Full control
%SystemRoot%\system32\Nbtstat.exe	Administrators: Full control
%SystemRoot%\system32\Net.exe	Administrators: Full control
%SystemRoot%\system32\Net1.exe	Administrators: Full control
%SystemRoot%\system32\Netsh.exe	Administrators: Full control
%SystemRoot%\system32\Netstat.exe	Administrators: Full control
%SystemRoot%\system32\Nslookup.exe	Administrators: Full control
%SystemRoot%\system32\Ntbackup.exe	Administrators: Full control
%SystemRoot%\system32\Ntsd.exe	Administrators: Full control
%SystemRoot%\system32\Pathping.exe	Administrators: Full control
%SystemRoot%\system32\Ping.exe	Administrators: Full control
%SystemRoot%\system32\Print.exe	Administrators: Full control
%SystemRoot%\system32\Query.exe	Administrators: Full control
%SystemRoot%\system32\Rasdial.exe	Administrators: Full control
%SystemRoot%\system32\Rcp.exe	Administrators: Full control
%SystemRoot%\system32\Recover.exe	Administrators: Full control
%SystemRoot%\system32\Regedit.exe	Administrators: Full control
%SystemRoot%\system32\Regedt32.exe	Administrators: Full control
%SystemRoot%\system32\Regini.exe	Administrators: Full control
%SystemRoot%\system32\Register.exe	Administrators: Full control
%SystemRoot%\system32\Regsvr32.exe	Administrators: Full control
%SystemRoot%\system32\Replace.exe	Administrators: Full control

(continued)

File	Baseline Permissions
%SystemRoot%\system32\Reset.exe	Administrators: Full control
%SystemRoot%\system32\Rexec.exe	Administrators: Full control
%SystemRoot%\system32\Route.exe	Administrators: Full control
%SystemRoot%\system32\Routemon.exe	Administrators: Full control
%SystemRoot%\system32\Router.exe	Administrators: Full control
%SystemRoot%\system32\Rsh.exe	Administrators: Full control
%SystemRoot%\system32\Runas.exe	Administrators: Full control
%SystemRoot%\system32\Runonce.exe	Administrators: Full control
%SystemRoot%\system32\Secedit.exe	Administrators: Full control
%SystemRoot%\system32\Setpwd.exe	Administrators: Full control
%SystemRoot%\system32\Shadow.exe	Administrators: Full control
%SystemRoot%\system32\Share.exe	Administrators: Full control
%SystemRoot%\system32\Snmp.exe	Administrators: Full control
%SystemRoot%\system32\Snmptrap.exe	Administrators: Full control
%SystemRoot%\system32\Subst.exe	Administrators: Full control
%SystemRoot%\system32\Telnet.exe	Administrators: Full control
%SystemRoot%\system32\Termsrv.exe	Administrators: Full control
%SystemRoot%\system32\Tftp.exe	Administrators: Full control
%SystemRoot%\system32\Tlntadmin.exe	Administrators: Full control
%SystemRoot%\system32\Tlntsess.exe	Administrators: Full control
%SystemRoot%\system32\Tlntsvr.exe	Administrators: Full control
%SystemRoot%\system32\Tracert.exe	Administrators: Full control
%SystemRoot%\system32\Tree.com	Administrators: Full control
%SystemRoot%\system32\Tsadmin.exe	Administrators: Full control
%SystemRoot%\system32\Tscon.exe	Administrators: Full control
%SystemRoot%\system32\Tsdiscon.exe	Administrators: Full control
%SystemRoot%\system32\Tskill.exe	Administrators: Full control
%SystemRoot%\system32\Tsprof.exe	Administrators: Full control
%SystemRoot%\system32\Tsshutdn.exe	Administrators: Full control
%SystemRoot%\system32\Usrmgr.com	Administrators: Full control
%SystemRoot%\system32\Wscript.exe	Administrators: Full control
%SystemRoot%\system32\Xcopy.exe	Administrators: Full control

Appendix B

Default Windows 2000 Services

The Default column shows the service startup for a Windows 2000-based server. The Baseline column shows the configure startup for each service after the Member Server Baseline Policy is applied.

Service	Full Name	Default	Baseline
Alerter	Alerter	Automatic	Disabled
AppMgmt	Application Management	Manual	Disabled
ClipSrv	ClipBook	Manual	Disabled
EventSystem	COM+ Event System	Manual	Manual
Browser	Computer Browser	Automatic	Disabled
DHCP	DHCP Client	Automatic	Automatic
Dfs	Distributed File System	Automatic	Enabled only in the DC role
TrkWks	Distributed Link Tracking Client	Automatic	Automatic
TrkSrv	Distributed Link Tracking Server	Manual	Disabled
MSDTC	Distributed Transaction Coordinator	Automatic	Disabled
DNSCache	DNS Client	Automatic	Automatic
EventLog	Event Log	Automatic	Automatic
Fax	Fax Service	Manual	Disabled
NtFrs	File Replication	Manual	Disabled
IISADMIN	IIS Admin Service	Automatic	Disabled
Cisvc	Indexing Service	Manual	Disabled

(continued)

Service	Full Name	Default	Baseline
SharedAccess	Internet Connection Sharing	Manual	Disabled
IsmServ	Intersite Messaging	Disabled	Disabled
PolicyAgent	IPSEC Policy Agent(IPSEC Service)	Automatic	Disabled
Kdc	Kerberos Key Distribution Center	Disabled	Enabled only in the DC role
LicenseService	License Logging Service	Automatic	Disabled
Dmserver	Logical Disk Manager	Automatic	Automatic
Dmadmin	Logical Disk Manager Administrative Service	Manual	Manual
Messenger	Messenger	Automatic	Disabled
Netlogon	Net Logon	Automatic*	Automatic
Mnmsrvc	NetMeeting Remote Desktop Sharing	Manual	Disabled
Netman	Network Connections	Manual	Manual
NetDDE	Network DDE	Manual	Disabled
NetDDEdsdm	Network DDE DSDM	Manual	Disabled
NtLmSsp	NTLM Security Support Provider	Manual	Disabled
SysmonLog	Performance Logs and Alerts	Manual	Manual
PlugPLay	Plug and Play	Automatic	Automatic
Spooler	Print Spooler	Automatic	Enabled only in the File and Print role
ProtectedStorage	Protected Storage	Automatic	Automatic
RSVP	QoS Admission Control (RSVP)	Manual	Disabled
RasAuto	Remote Access Auto Connection Manager	Manual	Disabled
RasMan	Remote Access Connection Manager	Manual	Disabled
RpcSs	Remote Procedure Call (RPC)	Automatic	Automatic
Rpclocator	Remote Procedure Call (RPC) Locator	Manual	Enabled only in the DC role
RemoteRegistry	Remote Registry Service	Automatic	Automatic
NtmsSvc	Removable Storage	Automatic	Disabled
RemoteAccess	Routing and Remote Access	Disabled	Disabled

Service	Full Name	Default	Baseline
Seclogon	RunAs Service	Automatic	Disabled
SamSs	Security Accounts Manager	Automatic	Automatic
Lanmanserver	Server	Automatic	Automatic
SMTPSVC	Simple Mail Transport Protocol (SMTP)	Automatic	Disabled
ScardSvr	Smart Card	Manual	Disabled
ScardDrv	Smart Card Helper	Manual	Disabled
SENS	System Event Notification	Automatic	Automatic
Schedule	Task Scheduler	Automatic	Disabled
LmHosts	TCP/IP NetBIOS Helper Service	Automatic	Automatic
TapiSrv	Telephony	Manual	Disabled
TlntSvr	Telnet	Manual	Disabled
TermService	Terminal Services	Disabled	Disabled
UPS	Uninterruptible Power Supply	Manual	Disabled
UtilMan	Utility Manager	Manual	Disabled
MSIServer	Windows Installer	Manual	Disabled
WinMgmt	Windows Management Instrumentation	Manual	Disabled
WMI	Windows Management Instrumentation Driver Extensions	Manual	Manual
W32Time	Windows Time	Automatic*	Automatic
LanmanWorkstation	WorkStation	Automatic	Automatic
W3svc	World Wide Web Publishing Service	Automatic	Enabled only in the IIS role

* - Automatic for a server in the domain. Manual if server belongs to a workgroup.

Appendix C

Additional Services

The following table lists additional services that are included with Windows 2000 Server and Advanced Server and can be added to a default installation.

Service	Full Name	Baseline
BINLSVC	Boot Information Negotiation Layer	Disabled
CertSvc	Certificate Services	Disabled
ClusSvc	Cluster Service	Disabled
DHCPServer	DHCP Server	Enabled only in the Infra role
DNS	DNS Server	Enabled only in the Infra and DC roles
MacFile	File Server for Macintosh	Disabled
MSFTPSVC	FTP Publishing Service	Disabled
NWCWorkstation	Gateway Service for Netware	Disabled
IAS	Internet Authentication Service	Disabled
MSMQ	Message Queuing	Disabled
NntpSvc	Network News Transport Protocol (NNTP)	Disabled
NSLService	On-Line Presentation Broadcast	Disabled
MacPrint	Print Server for Macintosh	Disabled
RSVP	QoS RSVP	Disabled
Remote_Storage_Engine	Remote Storage Engine	Disabled

(continued)

Service	Full Name	Baseline
Remote_Storage_File_System_Agent	Remote Storage File	Disabled
Remote_Storage_Subsystem	Remote Storage Media	Disabled
Remote_Storage_User_Link	Remote Storage Notification	Disabled
NwSapAgent	SAP Agent	Disabled
SimpTcp	Simple TCP/IP Services	Disabled
Groveler	Single Instance Storage Groveler	Disabled
LDAPSVCX	Site Server ILS Service	Disabled
SNMP	SNMP Service	Disabled
SNMPTRAP	SNMP Trap Service	Disabled
LPDSVC	TCP/IP Print Server	Disabled
TermServLicensing	Terminal Services Licensing	Disabled
TFTPD	Trivial FTP Daemon	Disabled
WINS	Windows Internet Name Service (WINS)	Enabled only in the Infra role
nsmonitor	Windows Media Monitor Service	Disabled
nsprogram	Windows Media Program Service	Disabled
nsstation	Windows Media Station Service	Disabled
nsunicast	Windows Media Unicast Service	Disabled

Job Aid 1:
Threat and Vulnerability Analysis Table

As new threats and vulnerabilities appear in your environment, you will need to establish the risk to your environment. This will help you ensure that the most critical threats are dealt with more promptly. Use the table below to record information about threats and vulnerabilities you face.

Threat: <Insert Threat Name here>

Threat <Threat Name>	
Threat Type	What is the nature of the threat or threats that you face?
Vulnerability	What vulnerability is exposed?
Exploit	How would a threat take advantage of the vulnerability?
Countermeasure	How do you counteract the threat to your environment?
Criticality	On a scale of 1-10 how critical is the threat?
Effort	On a scale of 1-10 how easy to exploit?
Risk Level	Criticality/Effort
Probability	Estimated percentage likelihood of threat happening?
Total Threat	Risk x Probability
Compromise Result	What happens when you are exploited?
Loss Exposure (estimated loss	Estimated financial loss
Exposure	Loss Exposure x Probability
Mitigation/Assignment	If you have to leave the vulnerability open how do you guard it effectively.
Incident Response	If you get compromised, what do you do?
Owner	Who is responsible?
Status	What state is the vulnerability in right now, "Closed", "Open", "Mitigated".
Software Version	What version is affected?

Job Aid 2:
Top Security Blunders

Even the latest technology and good overall IT Security staff can be foiled by uninformed or careless users. The list of blunders below is divided into events occurring at the client computer (or by the user) and those that occur at the server (or by the IT staff):

Top 11 Client-side Security Blunders

1. **Password Blunders**

   a. **Insecure passwords.** Users will naturally tend to select easy to remember (and therefore easy to crack) passwords. While you can enforce complex passwords through Windows 2000 Security Policies, ultimately password security depends upon each individual user. Passwords are often derived from names of children, pets, anniversary dates, or words from paraphernalia surrounding the work environment. Even worse, the actual password may be in plain view!

   b. **Sharing passwords between users.** Particularly in environments where users share computers, the users will often share passwords. This practice is very insecure and should be discouraged.

   c. **Using the internal organization password on external web sites.** If your users expose their password outside your organization, you're vulnerable to attack. User passwords are often stored with e-mail addresses. Using only that combination, an attacker can determine the organization for which the user works, the network user name (if it's the prefix of the SMTP address), and the password for the user.

2. **Failure to adequately perform backups and/or storing vital information locally rather than centrally.** In many organizations, client computers (especially laptops) are not backed up. Storing information locally on client computers, rather than on managed servers, can make recovery of data after an attack is virtually impossible.

3. **Open, unattended workstations.** Do you have a policy in place that encourages users to lock their workstations when they leave them? If not, a passerby could easily set up means to access that workstation after hours (for example by installing terminal server, PC Anywhere, or escalating local privilege).

4. **Ignoring vendor updates and patches.** All software and hardware has vulnerabilities and is in a continuous state of development. Feature improvements, design improvements, and bug fixes will generally be released until the software is no longer useful. Because software and (to a lesser extent) hardware is constantly changing, it is imperative that the IT staff stay current on patches, updates and fixes to their systems. Failure to remain current puts the attacker at an advantage.

5. **Not physically securing computer equipment.** Equipment, especially laptops, is a frequent target of theft. A laptop in the hands of an attacker, especially a laptop owned by a user with significant access to systems, can be a serious security threat.

6. **Disabling or diminishing existing security controls.** Users often attempt to disable virus protection in hopes of faster processing speeds. Additionally, to achieve greater convenience, they lower or remove macro security protection on productivity applications such as Microsoft Word, Microsoft Excel, and so on. It is important to educate users on the importance of maintaining security controls.

7. **Installing unnecessary and/or unapproved software.** Users prone to installing unauthorized or unapproved software place the organization at risk by potentially executing applications containing Trojan Horses or other vehicles of security compromise.

8. **Exposing more personal information than necessary.** Sharing names of children, full birthdates, and so on, enables attackers more opportunity to either guess passwords or acquire unauthorized access by means of social engineering. Information may be shared directly—verbally to the attackers over the phone, through e-mail, or passively by what is stored in the work area (pictures of children, information containing their social security number, health cards, and so on.)

9. **Propagating virus and other hoaxes.** False viruses and warnings that are mass distributed through e-mail cost money and time in their own right. You should ensure that your users send this information directly to the IT department rather than distributing it around the organization.

10. **Opening unexpected e-mail attachments.** Fostering a conservative cautious approach to receiving and opening attachments goes a long way towards preventing security incidents.

11. **Failure to train users to recognize security incidents and how to respond.** Many incidents could be mitigated or avoided if users were properly trained to recognized signs of attack, misconfiguration, virus, or other incidents. They also must be trained to properly respond once they have recognized an attack.

Top 8 Server-side Security Blunders

1. **Password Blunders**
   a. **Insecure passwords.** IT staff members often safeguard themselves from a lockout by creating backdoors. Passwords for these backdoors are generally simpler, easier to remember and consequently less secure. While this situation can partially be mitigated by implementing and enforcing Windows 2000 Security Policies, you must ensure users with high-level access are actually subject to Group Policy.
   b. **Sharing passwords between IT staff.** For example, allowing more than one user access to the Administrator account will make auditing and account-ability difficult or impossible should a security event occur involving that account. Users, especially IT staff, must have individual, auditable responsi-bility for their accounts. Prohibition of sharing passwords should be part of security policy signed by the users and IT staff.
   c. **Using the internal organization password on external web sites.** If your users expose their password outside your organization, you're vulnerable to attack. User's passwords are often stored with their e-mail addresses. Using only that combination, an attacker can determine where the user works, their user name (especially if it's the prefix of the SMTP address), and their password.

2. **Failure to implement all levels of the defense-in-depth strategy.** While it is important to implement and correctly configure a firewall and an intrusion detection system, security countermeasures must not stop there. For example, your defense-in-depth strategy should specify administrative and personnel-level controls. Many companies fail to adequately train public facing individuals such as receptionists and telephone operators to recognize and protect sensitive information. Failure to adequately protect against all layers of potential attack is a common mistake that leads to a false sense of security. For more information on defense-in-depth, see "Chapter 2" of this guide.

3. **Failure to consistently perform and validate system backups.** Many organiza-tions, including large organizations, fail to adequately back up important system data. Of the few that actually perform back ups, not many take the time to restore a file or otherwise validate the success of each back up operation. This can lead to situations where entire sets of backup media have gone bad and cannot be used to restore data lost to an attack or catastrophic failure.

4. **Running unnecessary services.** Default installations often enable more services than necessary for operation. These additional services provide more avenues for potential attacks and must be disabled. Only necessary services should be running. Services should periodically be audited to ensure need for them still exists.

5. **Not recognizing internal security threats.** A natural tendency is to focus security efforts and resources towards attacks from outside the organization. Sometimes this tendency results in a lack of focus on the bigger potential threat—people inside your organization. Whether intentional or unintentional, people on the inside of your organization have the most access and therefore pose the greatest potential threat for damage.

6. **Failure to consistently enforce security policy.** An excellent security policy only loosely enforced will have little benefit to the organization. Loosely enforcing security policy also has the dangerous side effect of creating apathy among employees towards security.

7. **Granting more privilege to services than necessary.** Services need a certain level of access in order to perform their specific tasks within the context of the system. When installing or troubleshooting these services, it may be tempting to grant more access than necessary in order to achieve functionality quickly. Services must have the least amount of privilege possible in order to maintain system security. You should ensure that this is enforced by both system administrators who configure service privilege, and application developers who create service dependencies.

8. **Failure to adequately harden applications developed in-house.** In-house applications should have the same or higher scrutiny as third-party applications.

Job Aid 3:
Attacks and Countermeasures

Technical Vulnerability Exploitation	Specific Countermeasures	Standard Countermeasures											
		Enforce Complex Passwords	Enable Logging/Auditing	Review System Configuration	Disable Services	Implement Intrusion Detection System	Data Encryption	Digital Signatures	Implement a Firewall	Application Hardening	Maintain Updated Vendor Patches	Security Policies and Procedures	Implement Tripwires
Password cracking	Use highest possible levels of encryption.	✓	✓	✓	✓	✓	✓					✓	
Buffer overflows	Force OS and applications to validate size and preferably type of data they accept. Use application level firewall.			✓	✓	✓			✓	✓	✓		
Network sniffing	Restrict local network connectivity and hardware controls. Use sniffer detection tools.			✓	✓	✓	✓					✓	
Replay attacks	Establish one-time passwords, prevent packet sniffing			✓	✓			✓					
Session hijacking	Eliminate predictable TCP sequence numbers, Implement SSL, force cookies, and prevent local network connectivity.					✓	✓	✓	✓				

Technical Vulnerability Exploitation	Specific Countermeasures	Enforce Complex Passwords	Enable Logging/Auditing	Review System Configuration	Disable Services	Implement Intrusion Detection System	Data Encryption	Digital Signatures	Implement a Firewall	Application Hardening	Maintain Updated Vendor Patches	Security Policies and Procedures	Implement Tripwires
Information gathering	Restrict direct access by using a proxy-based firewall, implement an intelligent intrusion detection system that can update filtering devices, require authentication prior to access to applications, and segregate security domains with firewalls.		✓	✓	✓	✓			✓		✓		
Document grinding (electronic dumpster diving)	Review all publicly available information for adherence to security policies. For example, how many specific user e-mails can be ascertained from the public web site? Are these e-mails directly correlated to user accounts?											✓	
Wireless leak	Reduce wireless connectivity zone, implement hardware restrictions, and use multifactor authentication.			✓		✓	✓						
Social engineering	Implement strong policies and training program.											✓	

Technical Vulnerability Exploitation	Specific Countermeasures	Standard Countermeasures											
		Enforce Complex Passwords	Enable Logging/Auditing	Review System Configuration	Disable Services	Implement Intrusion Detection System	Data Encryption	Digital Signatures	Implement a Firewall	Application Hardening	Maintain Updated Vendor Patches	Security Policies and Procedures	Implement Tripwires
Denial of Service & Distributed Denial of Service Attacks	Collect baselines to define normal service levels. All access should be granted with least privilege. Apply Network Ingress filtering to reduce IP-spoofed packets. (see RFC 2267 for details). Implement router filters, enable quota systems, monitor system performance, monitor Distributed Denial of Service attack signatures using an intrusion detection system implement fault tolerance and load balancing solutions. Implement TCP/IP stack improvements according to vendor.			✓		✓			✓		✓		
Cookie exploitation	For cookie implementers: include the least amount of information possible, NEVER use plain text to store information in cookies, use specific paths when possible.			✓		✓					✓		

Technical Vulnerability Exploitation	Specific Countermeasures	Enforce Complex Passwords	Enable Logging/Auditing	Review System Configuration	Disable Services	Implement Intrusion Detection System	Data Encryption	Digital Signatures	Implement a Firewall	Application Hardening	Maintain Updated Vendor Patches	Security Policies and Procedures	Implement Tripwires
CGI attacks	Ensure your CGI scripts dynamically handle various user input size, never pass unchecked remote user input to a shell command, consider using a CGI wrapper.									✓	✓		✓
DNS poisoning	Use Secure DNS (SDNS) and implement a split DNS that uses a trusted internal and an untrusted external DNS. Both may be on the same firewall. Restrict and authenticate Zone transfers.			✓		✓			✓	✓	✓		✓
E-mail spoofing	Use digital signatures or certificates. Prevent mail relaying or spoofing on SMTP servers.			✓		✓		✓					
IP spoofing	Apply Network Ingress filtering (see RFC 2827 for details).			✓		✓			✓	✓	✓		
Viruses	Train end users to identify virus behavior and proper response, prevent disabling of virus detection software, force timely virus signature updates. Only use trusted software.		✓	✓				✓			✓	✓	✓

Standard Countermeasures

Technical Vulnerability Exploitation	Specific Countermeasures	Enforce Complex Passwords	Enable Logging/Auditing	Review System Configuration	Disable Services	Implement Intrusion Detection System	Data Encryption	Digital Signatures	Implement a Firewall	Application Hardening	Maintain Updated Vendor Patches	Security Policies and Procedures	Implement Tripwires
Worms	Train end users to identify virus behavior and proper response, prevent disabling of virus detection software, force timely virus signature updates.		✓	✓	✓	✓			✓	✓	✓	✓	✓
Trojans	Train end users to identify virus behavior and proper response, prevent disabling of virus detection software, force timely virus signature updates. Only use trusted software.		✓	✓				✓			✓	✓	✓
Insider abuse	The insider threat is the hardest to reduce or remove. Implement strong policies, separation of duties, privilege restrictions, peer review, job rotation, and intrusion detection system.	✓	✓	✓	✓	✓	✓	✓	✓	✓	✓	✓	✓
Accidental deletion or misconfiguration of services	Limit scope of authority (only log on with Enterprise Admin or Domain Admin permissions when necessary) Readily available, current backups mitigate Fat finger mistakes. Implement a strong training program and where necessary a peer review program.	✓	✓									✓	✓

Job Aid 4:
Incident Response
Quick Reference Card

Using the following checklist as a guideline will help ensure you complete the necessary steps to respond to incidents effectively. However, the exact order of the steps will depend upon the nature of your organization and the incident. For more details on Incident Response, see Chapter 7 "Responding to Incidents."

General Guidelines for Incident Response
Document everything. Consider taping your comments. Note who did what, when, and why.
Keep your head. Resist the tendency to overreact or panic. Methodically follow security policy.
Use out of band communication such as telephone, fax, and face to face communication. Your attacker may be able to listen in.
Stay in constant communication across teams, and other impacted individuals.
Avoid restarting the computer, logging on and off, or otherwise inadvertently starting malicious code.

Objective 1 – Make Initial Assessment	
1.1	Contact technical team to ensure incident is not a false positive.
1.2	Examine audit logs for unusual activity, absence of logs or gap in logs.
1.3	Look for hacker tools (password cracking tools, Trojan horses, and so on.)
1.4	Check for unauthorized applications configured to start automatically.
1.5	Examine accounts for increased privilege or unauthorized group members.
1.6	Check for unauthorized processes.
1.7	Determine if evidence will be preserved.
1.8	Match compromised system performance against baseline.
1.9	Assign an initial priority level and an incident lead.

Objective 2 – Communicate the Incident

2.1	Communicate the incident to appropriate stakeholders and CSIRT liaisons.

Objective 3 – Contain the Damage and Minimize Risk

3.1	Depending on severity and security policy, isolate the affected systems by taking them offline.
3.2	Change passwords on affected systems.
3.3	Back up systems for recovery and, if appropriate, collecting evidence.

Objective 4 – Identify Type and Severity of Compromise(s)

4.1	Determine type of attack.
4.2	Determine intent of attack (specifically directed at your organization, automated attack, information gathering)
4.3	Identify all systems involved in attack. Revisit containment steps if additional systems are identified.
4.4	Reevaluate and, if necessary, reassign priority level to event.

Objective 5 – Protect Evidence

5.1	Back up systems with media never before used as early as possible in the response and recover cycle.
5.2	If possible, back up entire systems, including logs and system state.
5.3	Maintain provable chain of custody for evidence collected.
5.4	Secure evidence and document who collected, how, when, and who had access to it.

Objective 6 – Notify External Agencies

6.1	Under legal counsel direction, notify local and/or federal law enforcement.
6.2	Inform the CSIRT public relations liaison of the outcome, and assist as necessary.
6.3	Notify other appropriate agencies such as the CERT Coordination Center at Carnegie Mellon University (http://www.cert.org). CERT and other such agencies can provide valuable recovery information.

Objective 7 – Recover Systems

7.1	Locate and validate most recent noncompromised backups.
7.2	Restore system.
7.3	Validate functionality and match system performance against historical baselines.
7.4	Monitor for repeat attack and misconfigurations due to containment steps.

Objective 8 – Compile and Organize Incident Documentation	
8.1	Compile all notes, recordings, into a comprehensive security incident activity log.
8.2	Distribute to incident participants for review and approval. (Including legal for evidentiary fitness).
8.3	Review cause of breach and improve defense to prevent it and related attacks in the future.
8.4	Assist finance department in assessing cost of breach.
8.5	Prepare report to management and other stakeholders to explain how the event occurred, the cost of the breach, and how it will be prevented in the future.

Index

notes

System state — contain registry data, plus all of the objects in AD

notes

notes

notes

notes

notes

notes

notes

notes

notes

notes

notes